Religions in America

A Guide for Evangelical Christians' Understanding and Witnessing

Robert F. Simms

To an Unnamed student
at Wake Forest University,
who tried to get me to become
a Mormon, and failed miserably,
but made me want to know more
about other religions, for the
encounters yet to come.

Religions in America

A Guide for
Evangelical Christians'
Understanding
and Witnessing

Robert F. Simms

Unless otherwise indicated, quotations from the Bible are from
the King James Version.

ISBN: 978-1-7378117-3-2
Published in the United States by
Robert F. Simms
Greer, South Carolina

Contents

Purpose of This Book

A college course in world religions would approach its subject in a purely academic way. It would present a history of the development of those religions, a survey of their beliefs, and perhaps a description of social and cultural effects brought about in lands where those religions have prevailed.

This little volume will accomplish some of those purposes, although to a lesser extent—a book of this size is obviously not exhaustive! But this book will go further than the realm of the academic. Our purpose is to introduce Evangelical Christians to the major religions in America, to give a defense of Christianity by comparison, and to provide helpful information with which Christians can discuss their own beliefs with persons who hold to another religious faith.

> **Our purpose is to introduce Evangelical Christians to the major religions in America, to give a defense of Christianity, and to provide helpful information with which Christians can discuss their own beliefs with persons of other religions.**

Further, the target audience for this book is Evangelical Protestant Christians, because of their interest in understanding persons of other religions with a view to presenting the gospel to them.

The reader who has browsed the table of contents has already discovered that the book includes a chapter describing the main doctrines of the Roman Catholic Church. In fact, because of alphabetical order, it's the first chapter. The first page or so of that chapter explains the reason for its inclusion, in view of the fact that many Protestants would agree that Catholicism, while very different from Protestantism, is undeniably Christian in essence.

One or two other religious groups could have been included that were not. The reason is almost entirely due to the number of adherents in America.

A chapter could have been devoted to Orthodox Christianity,

which comprises Greek Orthodox, Russian Orthodox, and other related Orthodox bodies. All these groups together, however, constitute only about 0.5% of Americans.

Shintoism, Sikhism, Taoism, Zoroastrianism, and any number of other esoteric groups could have been described, but all together they do not constitute a significant draw on the interests of many Americans.

Similarly, though the quasi-religious "life technique" of Scientology could have been discussed, estimates are that it claims only about 40,000 adherents worldwide.[1] Most Christians will never meet anyone who is a Scientologist.

We have chosen here to spotlight ten religions, some of which are less formally organized than others. And we present them in alphabetical order instead of by size or any valuation of significance.

---

[1] "Scientology," Wikipedia, October 18, 2023. https://en.wikipedia.org/wiki/Scientology.

Catholicism
A Church in Control
(Matthew 16:16-19)

During the 1960 U.S. Presidential campaign one of the key issues for vast numbers of Protestants—and probably some people of other faiths or no faith at all—was whether or not a Catholic should be the President of the United States. John Kennedy was Roman Catholic. In private conversations, an oft-repeated objection to his election was that Kennedy might obey the Pope, and the Pope shouldn't control America. As unlikely as it might have seemed to some then, or to most of us today, that fear was widespread.

In the political world of the 21st century, a similar fear is expressed by many people about elected officials who espouse especially conservative Christian faith in general—that they will mix religion and politics. The fear is alarmist, and certainly prejudicial.

The concept of control, however, is the significant thing that characterizes the Roman Catholic Church. This control is multifaceted. This chapter will inspect the kinds of control Catholicism exerts throughout its hierarchy.

Explanatory Note

Other than in this particular chapter, this book deals with non-Christian religions, including those that make a claim to being Christian but are not. Some persons would not consider it appropriate in such a work to deal with Catholicism, its being commonly classified as a major branch of Christianity. And some readers of this book will have family connections to Roman Catholicism or other reasons to be either sensitive or on guard about it. But the differences between Catholicism and Protestantism are so great, and those between Catholics and Evangelical Protestants particularly so immense, that a treatment of the Roman Church as being nearly as distinct as if it were another religion is fully warranted.

For our purposes then, the author concedes that Roman Catholicism is a major branch of genuine Christianity. It is our purpose to describe how its major tenets differ from Evangelical Protestantism, and to suggest what Evangelicals can do to communicate their faith perspectives to Roman Catholic friends.

Scriptural starting point

In any discussion of Catholicism, from whatever viewpoint, the Bible text that quickly crops up is from Matthew's gospel, a memorable event during the ministry of Jesus:

> **"Simon Peter answered, "You are the Messiah, the Son of the living God."**
>
> **Jesus replied, "Blessed are you, Simon son of Jonah, for this was not revealed to you by flesh and blood, but by my Father in heaven. And I tell you that you are Peter, and on this rock I will build my church, and the gates of Hades will not overcome it. I will give you the keys of the kingdom of heaven; whatever you bind on earth will be bound in heaven, and whatever you loose on earth will be loosed in heaven"(Matthew 16:16-19 NIV).**

Jesus said he would build his church on the strong, divinely revealed confession of his being the Christ, the Son of God. The Catholic Church has perpetuated a misinterpretation of these verses that has resulted in its exclusive approach to salvation, revelation, and church itself. Due to its unique ecclesiology, Catholicism is deeply interested in maintaining control over many things.

Control of Churches

The Catholic Church is first a church in control of churches—its individual congregations. Catholics believe in a universal church—in fact, the word *catholic* simply means "universal." To the most orthodox Catholic there is no other church but the Roman Catholic Church, and it is composed of all the local parishes and dioceses. The hierarchy of bishops, whom the Catholic Church considers the successors of Peter and the Apostles, and whose head is the Bishop of Rome, controls the Church.

In the first three centuries of Christianity, this was not the way the original church[2] functioned. The bishop (or, pastor) of the local church was accorded the highest leadership for that congregation. The larger churches had prominent pastors, and not only would their own congregations consult them on matters of concern, but smaller churches and their pastors might request the help or arbitration of more established churches. Paul's letters indicate that the church at Rome had distinguished itself as such a leading body. But until the middle of A.D. 300 there was no hierarchy of churches or bishops. The churches were autonomous, though cooperative. But as the church at Rome grew, the Bishop of Rome magnified his accorded status.

In A.D. 313 the Roman Empire legalized Christianity, after nearly three centuries of persecution, and in A.D. 380 it became the Empire's official religion—thus, the "Holy Roman Empire." With this development, the church at Rome was on a path to control of all the churches in the Empire.

The Roman church maintained that Christ had given to Peter, himself, the keys to the Church, making him head of all the other apostles and their churches. Further, the Roman church claimed that Peter had been the Bishop of the church at Rome for 25 years. On that basis, the Bishop of Rome pressed for authority over all the other bishops.

There is no significant evidence for the claim that Peter was

---

[2] In this chapter in particular, the word "church," not capitalized and not connected with "Roman" or "Catholic," means the early church as begun at the first Christian Pentecost and not organized into any hierarchy.

ever even associated with the church at Rome—Paul, yes, but not Peter. Nevertheless when the first universal counsel was held in A.D. 325, the Roman church pressed its claim, and when the canons were issued from that counsel, the Roman church forged into its copy of the canons the phrasing of its superiority. The forgery was later discovered, but by then the idea had done its damage.[3]

When the Roman Empire moved its capital to Constantinople in the A.D. 330s, the Bishop of Rome was free to develop his status. In the A.D. 400s, Innocent I and Leo kept up the campaign, finally securing imperial recognition of the primacy of the Bishop of Rome, but only after several more forgeries and political maneuvers were executed. Throughout the middle ages, nothing was more jealously guarded and devotedly cultivated as the authority of the Bishop of Rome, who came to be known as Papa—Father, or simply, the Pope.

It is vital to remember, however, that the Catholic church was not truly universal. The churches that lay roughly east of Rome developed their own traditions and hierarchy and eventually split with the western churches. The eastern churches became the Eastern Orthodox Church and the western churches became the Roman Catholic Church. Their separation became official in A.D. 1054.

Even within the western, Roman Catholic Church there were always groups here and there that were not under the control of the hierarchy. Typically, these were churches on the outlying areas of the empire that dated back to early missionary ventures of the church, and which had never given up their autonomous character in order to take direction from the Bishop of Rome. The British Isles were among those places where independent groups survived. As well, there were always groups of believers who dissented under the dictates of their conscience, not being able to accept the

---

[3] Robert Baker, *A Summary of Christian History* (Nashville: Broadman Press, 1959), 72.

church as they found it. Such groups as the Huguenots and the Jansenists in France were among the larger movements of dissent, and they felt the persecuting wrath of the Roman Catholic church in return, as she attempted to squelch all differing opinions and take control of churches everywhere (at least in the west).

What was the rock to which Jesus referred? It was not Peter himself, but the rock-solid conviction he had just expressed, the foundational truth that would underlie every genuine Christian's faith and every genuine church's existence: "You are the Christ, the Son of the Living God.

All this control they based principally on Matthew 16:18, where Jesus said to Peter, "You are Peter, and on this rock I will build my church... I will give you the keys of the kingdom of heaven." But what does this verse say? The Greek from which it is translated contains a play on words, as does the Aramaic, which Jesus no doubt spoke to Peter. He said, "You are Peter (Gk. *petros*), and on this rock *(petra)* I will build my church. Peter's name is a *masculine* noun, but "rock" is a *feminine* noun—hence, the play on words.

Most people know that the name Peter means *Rock* but technically it means something more like "Man of the Rock." But what was the rock to which Jesus referred? It was not Peter himself, but the rock-solid conviction he had just expressed, the foundational truth that would underlie every genuine Christian's faith and every genuine church's existence: "You are the Christ, the Son of the Living God." The word also alludes to the Old Testament references to the coming Messiah as the Rock. The Psalmist called his Lord his Rock (e.g. Psalm 19:4). And later, Paul would write in 1 Corinthians 10:4, "that rock was Christ." Jesus did *not* mean that Peter was the rock that the coming church would be built upon. For the first two centuries of the church, its ministers and members understood this truth.

Christ meant his church would be built on the confession that he was the Savior, the Son of God—the Rock of our Salvation. The keys of the kingdom Jesus referred to in this verse likewise do not indicate that Peter was set up as superior to the other apostles. Listen to what A. T. Robertson, renowned Greek scholar, says on this portion of the verse:

> ...We do not understand it as a special and peculiar prerogative belonging to Peter. The same power here given to Peter belongs to every disciple of Jesus in all the ages. Advocates of papal supremacy insist on the primacy of Peter here and in the power of Peter to pass on this supposed sovereignty to others. But this is all quite beside the mark. We soon see the disciples actually disputing again as to which of them is the greatest in the kingdom of heaven... Clearly neither Peter nor the rest understood Jesus to say here that Peter was to have supreme authority. What is added shows that Peter held the keys precisely as every preacher and teacher does... Every preacher uses the keys of the kingdom when he proclaims the terms of salvation in Christ. The proclamation of these terms when accepted by faith in Christ has the sanction and approval of God the Father.[4]

It is not surprising, however, that the Bishop of Rome would hold the opinion that Jesus gave Peter and his designees supremacy over the church. By the fourth century, Christianity in general had come to accept several non-scriptural propositions including the idea of the universal church being principally composed of the bishops, the phenomenon of a special priesthood qualified by ordination to administer sacraments, and an episcopal form of government. Baker's book on church history adds that

---

[4] A. T. Robertson, *Word Pictures in the New Testament, Vol. 1* (Nashville: Broadman Press, 1930), 134-35.

"one of the most important reasons for the rise of the Roman bishop is the type of men who held the office. They recognized the dignity of their position and sought in every way to forward it. As evidenced by the forgery mentioned heretofore, they wanted first place and actively sought it."[5]

In Control of Doctrine

One chief aim of the control sought by the early bishops, and Rome in particular, and for the control still guarded today, is that the Catholic Church should define and mandate doctrinal beliefs.

The unwavering official position of the Roman Catholic Church is that it is the teaching authority for all Roman Catholics. The bishops in parishes everywhere teach what has been determined by the hierarchy, which is headed by the Pope. If they do not, they can be disciplined, which ultimately may mean being defrocked.

From the earliest church councils the major reason for their convening was to wrangle with divergent doctrinal views as they developed. Granted, these councils enabled the early church to deal with major heresies in an authoritative way, and what the early church determined in those councils often settled matters of theological orthodoxy for not only Catholics at the time, but also for most Protestants later. But such councils also left a legacy of doctrinal control that has fed Catholic ecclesiastical power-structures through the centuries. For the issue of the primacy of the Roman bishop was not principally about the day-to-day decisions made in each church, but about the very core activities of those churches: their preaching and teaching of the doctrine of Christ.

The Roman church's position was and still is that the Bishop of Rome is the successor to Peter, and as such is the recipient of

---

[5] Baker, *Summary*, 72-3.

the supreme authority to interpret the scriptures, and to teach the church. Crucial to this claim is the corollary claim that the Pope in matters of doctrine is incapable of making error, because God keeps him from it. This is known as the doctrine of papal infallibility.

While the Roman Church promulgated this belief informally from the middle ages onward, it was not formally adopted until the First Vatican Council (1869-1870). The doctrine does not mean that the Pope is perfect, but only that in his official teaching ministry—anything he speaks *ex cathedra*—he never leads the church astray.

Under this system of authority, the Catholic Church has come to teach officially such doctrines as these:

Scriptures

The Catholic position is that the Bible is one of *two* sources accepted as authoritative for the Church. The other source is sacred tradition as preserved in the edicts of the church itself. Because of this belief, many Catholic views—such as the veneration of Mary, infant baptism and the existence of Purgatory—are based not on the Bible but on non-canonical writings including the apocrypha, statements of early church fathers, and encyclicals of one sort or another throughout the centuries.

Priesthood

1 Peter 2:9 says God made all believers a kingdom of priests, that all of us are possessors of the privilege of representing God before men and interceding for men before God. But the Catholic church holds to a restricted priesthood. The authority not only to rule the church, but also to dictate orthodox belief, is invested in priests, who themselves must be ordained by the church.

The average Catholic is not encouraged to study the Bible on his own. The historic absence of the word of God in the hands of the commoner is the direct result of the Roman Church's jealousy over the privilege of the priests alone to teach and interpret Scripture. From the time the Church (principally Jerome) translated the Hebrew and Greek scriptures into Latin in the 4th century, until nearly the time of the Protestant Reformation, the Latin Vulgate was the authoritative scripture of the Catholic Church, and knowledge of it was all but officially restricted to Church officials and priests.

Faith For the Catholic

"Faith is a free intellectual assent to whatever God reveals is true… What we are looking for, then, is the 'rule of faith,' that guide which will define exactly the content of divine revelation. For Catholics this rule of faith is found in the Catholic Church."[6] This description of faith says nothing of the need of an individual to accept personally the Lordship of Christ, or to entrust himself to the saving power of God, as we understand the Bible to teach.

Grace

Grace is defined by the Catholic Church as "a supernatural, transient help given us by our Lord to enlighten our mind and strengthen our will in the performance of supernatural acts."[7] Note the word *transient*. This word is a key to the concept of grace for the Catholic, because, as we shall see presently, the church mediates this grace to its members, and so maintains control over it.

Sin

Sin, for the Catholic, is either venial or mortal. Mortal sin is that wrong thing done with full knowledge and willful consent. Venial sin is wrong done when the person is either ignorant of its sinfulness or is forced against his will to do it.

---

[6] George Brantl, *Catholicism* (New York, G. Braziller, 1961), 164, 158.
[7] Adolph Tanquerey, *The Spiritual Life* (Westminster, MD, The Newman Press, 1930), 66. —A common phrase found in numerous Catholic writings.

Purgatory

To die in mortal sin places one in Purgatory, which is for the purging of lives not yet ready for the perfection of heaven. There is no scriptural basis for the Catholic belief in Purgatory. (This is one of many Catholic doctrines that rely *not* on the Bible but only on Church edicts.)

Eucharist

What many Evangelical Christians know as the Lord's Supper (and some as Communion) is quite distant from Catholic Communion or the Eucharist. Perhaps to oversimplify a complicated doctrine, we shall say that Catholicism teaches that under the blessing of the priest, the specially prepared wafer of communion is changed into the actual body of Christ as the words of the Mass are spoken. (Mass means "body," and refers to the body of Christ. The term is generalized to refer to the worship time where the Eucharist is performed.) Mass "provides an actual transfusion of spiritual energy from God to man… Christ's body and blood are actually present…their accidents remain as they were. But their substance is transubstantiated."[8] The Second Vatican Council decreed that the Eucharist is "to perpetuate the sacrifice of the cross throughout the centuries…a paschal banquet in which Christ is consumed."

For the Catholic Church, the sacrifice of Christ would not continue to be productive without this sacramental re-enactment. In other words, to the Catholic the cross is not the finished work of Christ; it must continue through the Mass, and believers have to receive it repeatedly through the ritual. In other words, they eat God, not just figuratively but (as they believe) in actuality.

Mary

Protestants often think Catholics worship Mary. Officially, the

---

[8] Huston Smith, *The World's Religions* (San Francisco, Harper, 1991), 350.

Catholic position is that Mary is "venerated," revered over all other saints because of her unique position. However, they add that they believe that Mary was, herself, conceived without original sin, a belief they see as a necessity to Jesus' being born without sin. As well, they assert that Mary not only bore Jesus in her virginity, but remained a virgin afterward—that the brothers and sisters spoken of in the Bible were not Mary's children. The Church has also decreed that Mary was "assumed" into heaven, meaning that she did not die, and that she may be addressed in prayer so as to intercede for Christians before Christ. All this is without scriptural warrant, and much of it is contrary to scripture's intent. The result is a doctrine which, in practical terms, amounts to the worship of Mary, whether it is called such or not.

Other "saints"[9] receive similar though lesser treatment in a system of honor that elevates certain meritorious persons to a status in heaven higher than that of other Christians. In connection with Mary and the saints there is much image-adoration, and much attached superstition, for instance claims to having performed miracles of a strange sort. The recurring flurry of excitement in Catholicism over whether or not statues or paintings of Mary weep is an example of the tragic proportions of this superstition, and of the integral involvement of Church control in everything: the phenomenon must not be called a miracle unless the church rules that it is. A number of other doctrines that are approved by the church and taught rigorously to every member may be briefly mentioned.

Marriage, for instance, is a sacrament of the church—a means of receiving grace from God—and divorce is prohibited. Persons who separate are to remain celibate.

Children are to be raised as Catholics, even in marriages between Catholics and persons of other faiths.

---

[9] The Greek word usually translated "saint" in the New Testament is *hagios,* which means simply "holy one." It is used in nearly every New Testament letter to refer to all Christians, made holy by the Holy Spirit (Romans 15:16).

Officially, artificial birth control is not permitted, though a few "natural" methods are tolerated.

Abortion is unexceptionally prohibited.

Priests and nuns are required to be unmarried, on the basis of the preferred order of service to Christ supposedly taught by Paul. This is unquestionably an unscriptural requirement, and is refuted by numerous passages, including the interesting fact that Peter himself was married.

Catholics are required to confess sins before a priest, who alone is authorized to grant, on behalf of God, forgiveness of sins, by requiring some act of contrition of the person confessing. (Confession is one of the seven sacraments of the Catholic Church.)

The fact that the sanctity of marriage, the immorality of abortion on demand, and the validity of celibacy as a way of life are all biblical teachings is not at issue. What is at issue is the way in which the Catholic church uses these thing to coerce and maintain control over its members. Many Catholic requirements constitute a mountain of beliefs that were based in part on good ideas but that exaggerated a flaw, with no basis in solid, exegetical interpretation of the word of God.

It is no wonder that Martin Luther, the Protestant reformer, coming out of the Catholic tradition, felt overburdened with the multitude of errors and misled in the crucial matter of salvation, and made his cry *"sola scriptura!"*—only the scriptures! In that tradition Evangelicals agree. As dear as the opinions of great preachers and church figures are, only the Bible will be the Evangelical's written authority, and even then not as interpreted not by one man, or by one organization, but as commonly revealed through the Holy Spirit's enlightenment. Where Protestants differ in their understanding of an interpretation, every believer is accountable only to God.

This idea of individual autonomy before God, however, is foreign to Catholic thinking. The Catholic church not only exercises control over the church everywhere, and over doctrine as a whole, but over its people in particular.

In Control of Members

Clearly, the Roman Church does not rule every affair of its members, but in a way that is tremendously significant it controls the life of virtually every Catholic: To the believing Catholic, his very eternity is in the hands of the Church and its priests. Salvation, in the Catholic understanding, is provided for in the life and work of Jesus Christ, who died on the cross to atone for our sins, and rose from the grave to bring victory over death and hell. So far, so good. But, to the Catholic, bringing Christ's accomplished salvation into the life of the individual is not a matter of individual decision and faith, but a matter of participating in the full sacramental life of the church. And the priests control the sacraments. Thus, the salvation of the Catholic, in his belief, depends on the administration of sacraments.

Baptism
The first of these sacraments is Baptism. Catholics baptize their infants, believing that the ritual imparts the first grace from God that inclines the person toward God and restores supernatural life, which we are born without, being born in sin. If a baby is not sprinkled, or the person is never baptized later, he has no hope of salvation. Confirmation is the sacrament that strengthens the adolescent for life. It is administered only after a child has learned the catechism, a question-and-answer book on Catholic belief.

Mass
Mass, or Communion, is the sacrament through which, as the Church teaches, it imparts the actual body of Christ to worshipers. The Church teaches that without receiving the transient (not lasting) grace that comes through "eating Christ," he does not continue to be saved, but falls from grace. Withholding the sacrament places a Catholic in grave danger.

This sacrament is based on such Bible passages as John 6:51-58, Mark 14:22-25, and others, which most Protestants interpret as symbolic. Jesus said, "This is my body," in the same sense as he said, "I am the door."

If the indoctrination of the Church has been successful, the fear of excommunication, or of any interruption in the sacraments, is generally sufficient to maintain Church control over the orthodoxy of life and belief among its members.

Extreme Unction

At the end of life, "last rites," or Extreme Unction, is performed for the dying or just-dead. Catholics believe that the priest has authority to influence the direction of the departing spirit by his pronouncements and prayers. As with many other Catholic beliefs, Extreme Unction has no basis in the Bible.

Excommunication

For severe departure from the faith, or disobedience to church teachings, a Catholic may even be excommunicated, which means to be cut off from the sacraments. If the indoctrination of the Church has been successful, the fear of excommunication, or of any interruption in the sacraments, is generally sufficient to maintain Church control over the orthodoxy of life and belief among its members.

Catholicity

As explained previously, the basis for the belief that the church is authorized to exercise this control is the Catholic interpretation of Matthew 16:19, which is that the entranceway to heaven itself is kept by the Church, headed by the See of Peter (basically, the Vatican and the Pope). But we have already seen that the words of Jesus did not indicate any such idea. Nevertheless, to this day the Pope declares that union of all churches under Rome is the will of

God.

To the question whether or not Catholicism regards other forms of Christianity as capable of leading people to salvation, the Vatican II canons say: "The Spirit of Christ has not refrained from using them as a means of salvation which draw their efficacy from the very fullness of grace and truth entrusted to the Catholic Church... (but) ...it is through Christ's Catholic Church alone, which is the all embracing means of salvation, that the fullness of the means of salvation can be obtained."

To interpret the statement above, it means that Catholics believe that persons in other denominations may manage to find salvation, but only because of their 'spiritual ties' to the Catholic church; but in any case it will not be an abundant salvation, unless it comes through actual fellowship with the Roman Church itself, which they refer to as the "mother church."

Non-Catholics may find many Catholic beliefs odd or bizarre. Some Protestants, especially those farthest from the liturgical tradition—Lutheran and Episcopal churches are examples of liturgical bodies—may even be repulsed by Catholic exclusiveness. Evangelicals should have concern for their Roman Catholic friends, however, because of the system in which they are virtually caught, usually without recognition of their predicament.

Perhaps the average Evangelical Christian might wonder if any Roman Catholics are saved. The bottom-line answer would have to be Yes. Some are saved not because they were sprinkled, or because they take Mass, but because somehow, amid all the error of the Roman system, they have come to repent of sin, to personally trust Jesus Christ as their Savior, and have committed their lives to him as Lord. Many times Catholics come to a personal and saving knowledge of Christ not because of what they learned in their own church, but because of what has come across to them through friends, evangelistic meetings, reading books, or the influence of Protestant church ministries.

Some Catholics deny that they believe some of the things that classical Catholicism teaches, but most Catholics fail to realize that what they believe as members will not shape what Catholicism becomes, because the Catholic Church is under hierarchical and papal control, not congregational.

In some eras, the very continuation of the Roman system seemed dependent on the ability of the Church to control not only its members, but other people and institutions as well.

Control of its Environment

The Catholic Church historically has sought to control not only its doctrines and its members, but its environment as well. Very early on, from at least the fifth century, the Catholic Church sought to control its international environment. From the time when the Emperor made Christianity the official religion of the Roman world, Catholicism has left a legacy of social and political involvement designed to secure control over people and events. Thus it was that the persecuted church became the persecuting church in the middle ages, conducting inquisitions and suppressing dissenting Christian groups wherever it found them. It is shameful that any group calling itself Christian would do the things that were done to other Christians, to say nothing of unbelievers, in the name of Christ.

It is no secret today that the Vatican wields tremendous power in the world. This power is not due solely to the so-called spiritual element of its organization, but to the political and economic ties it has made to the governments of scores of nations through its uncounted resources of men and money. In the middle ages, the general belief that the Church held the power of life and death resulted in kings and princes bowing to the will of the Pope.

The present-day concern of Evangelical Christians, however, is for the spiritual destiny of millions of Catholics, who may or may not hear the true, life-changing gospel in their parish. Testimony after testimony from former Catholics who were saved through the witnessing efforts of some evangelical believer demonstrate that gospel ministry to Catholics is one of the greatest challenges of evangelistic missionary efforts today.

What should Evangelicals do to influence Catholic friends or relatives?

- *Prayer.* The first and most important step is prayer. God honors and answers prayer, and when they pray, Christians themselves become more likely to be God's instruments in the answers to those prayers.
- *Relationships.* Another important key is building relationships with Catholic acquaintances. Often, witnessing is more effective and more welcome when it takes place in an atmosphere of developed friendship. Evangelicals need to find out whether or not their Catholic friends have a personal knowledge of Jesus Christ through faith in him. Recognizing, however, that Catholics speak a different *language of faith* is vital. An Evangelical should depend on the scriptures for his convictions, and then communicate his beliefs in love.
- *Intentionality.* Intentional influence, not merely the haphazard sort, is vital. Evangelical Christians should invite Catholic friends to their churches. They should express their sense of joy and peace in the assurance of salvation through faith in Christ alone. They should pray for them, and keep praying for them.

A great gulf exists between the institution of the Catholic Church and the individual Catholic person. In one sense, the Catholic is the victim of his church, in bondage to its centuries-old, deeply-entrenched error. The Catholic needs spiritual freedom, and that freedom comes through truth. Jesus *is* that truth. Those who know the truth and have been made free by it must communicate that gospel truth with those who need it.

Christian Science
Delusions of the Mind
(Matthew 7:21-22)

No one likes to be sick. Consequently, man has tried many things in his quest to conquer disease. Some of his methods have been based on fact, reason, history, or science; some have not. Whether the attempt at curing disease is surgical, medicinal, therapeutic, holistic or psychological, the never-ending battle testifies to the persistent unwillingness of human beings to acquiesce to the illnesses that plague them. In our concern with health, therefore, we welcome remedies by instrument and medicine, but also of the mind and spirit. And if a miracle should come along, we would not turn it down.

Anything, however, can be exaggerated, including the dream of man to be healed of his diseases without having to resort to surgery or even medicine. A clear illustration of this desire in institutional form is the religion of Christian Science.

In 1821, Mary Baker was born in New Hampshire into a family of strict Calvinists. As a little girl, Mary showed tremendous obstinacy and tenacity, and she developed an emotional and nervous condition that resulted in her having fits and spells of an uncommon order. Her physical and emotional condition was mixed with religious elements. Mary claimed that when she was eight she heard a voice calling to her at night repeatedly, saying, "Mary, Mary, Mary." When she finally told her mother, she was advised to answer as little Samuel in the Old Testament: "Speak, Lord, for thy servant heareth." Once she had answered in this way, the voice ceased.

Mary was a bright girl intellectually, perhaps much brighter than others her age, and she was advised because of this inequity and her frequent emotional fits to stay out of school. She learned at home.

She was sickly from the first. Then again, she was living in a time when "it was the style... for girls and young women to be frail and weak and to faint upon the slightest provocation."[10] Her condition may indeed have gone beyond that, but for the reader the fashionableness of being sickly should be kept in mind. First her family, then she, sought cures of different sorts for her. It did not help that no one could say exactly what her problem was. How much of it was psychological cannot be known now, so long after the fact.

Her family tried doctors; most likely they attempted spiritism, as it came into vogue in the middle of the century, and finally Mary was sent to a sanitarium. She left there, however, and sought out a mesmerizer in Portland, Maine, about whom she had read. Their meeting was the first sign of a turning point in her life. He produced a "cure" by talking to her while massaging her head. She decided he was onto something, and she returned to New Hampshire to work on the idea. In the course of her experimentation, she discovered that many of her ailing friends would recover under a program of spiritual counsel and sugar pills. Her conclusion was that the truth had set them free.

On February 4, 1866, after a fall on ice and a return to her sickly condition, she was in bed, given up for dead by doctor and family alike, when she took up a Bible to read. At random, she read in Matthew 9 about Jesus' healing people, and she decided to try to simply "rise up and walk." To the amazement of all, she did.

Mary's life turned around. She immediately began to work at formalizing the idea of healing through a change of mind. She joined the Unitarian church, never having liked the strict Calvinism of her father. In 1870 she began work on the book *Science and Health,* and in 1879, upon completion of it, she officially began the Church of Christ Scientist. Her experience had burgeoned into a religion.

The Church of Christ Scientist is described by Mary Baker Eddy[11] in her writings as "a church designed to commemorate the

---

[10] Charles Potter, *The Faiths Men Live By* (New York, Prentice Hall, 1954) 273.

[11] Asa Gilbert Eddy was Mary Baker's third husband.

word and works of our Master, which should reinstate primitive Christianity and its lost element of healing." Can we take that definition at face value? What is Christian Science? How does it stand in the light of the authentic word of God

In answering these questions, consider a New Testament text that provides guidance in the matter:

Not everyone who says to me "Lord, Lord," will enter the kingdom of heaven, but only the one who does the will of my Father who is in heaven. Many will say to me on that day, "Lord, Lord, did we not prophesy in your name and in your name drive out demons, and perform many miracles?" Then I will tell them plainly, "I never knew you. Away from me, you evildoers" (Matthew 7:21-22 NIV).

This text has fascinated many Christians, who may try to assign an identity to the people in this verse who call out, "Lord, Lord." The Lord's target in this warning, however, is more general. Those who will say, "Lord, Lord," in the end are people who believe they are on the right track, who have been convinced at least in part by some impressive evidence like healing or miracles, and who are sincerely religious. All too clearly, however, the idea of this pronouncement of Jesus is that whoever these people are, they are on the *wrong* track. They have been convinced by evidence the source of which was not God, and by the rationalizing power of their own minds. Religious or not, even acting in what they believe is Jesus' name, they are not among the people who will enjoy the heavenly presence of God forever. Jesus said, "I never knew you: Away from me."

Christian Science is a religion that claims to be leading people to the *original way of Christ and healing*. In fact, however, it leads people away from Christ and promulgates an exclusive, philosophical interpretation of the Bible that obscures its true meaning; it hides the precious message of salvation. Many pseudo-

Christian alternatives to true, biblical Christianity exist in the world, and each has its own special twist. With Christian Science, it's delusions of the mind.

The Delusion of Being Christian

The chief delusion of followers of Christian Science is that they are Christians.

A familiar critique of Christian Science is that it is neither Christian nor scientific.[12] Despite the claims of its founder and its many practitioners and followers, Christian Science does not biblically qualify as a Christian group. A spokesman for the Church of Christ Scientist said a Christian Scientist practitioner is "one who accepts the practices and teachings of this church as it (sic) is found in the Bible and the Christian Science textbook, *Science and Health with Key to the Scriptures,* by Mrs. Eddy."[13] When those teachings are compared with the plain language of the Bible, Christian Science shows itself to be far from Christian.

Christian Science is neither Christian nor scientific.

God—A Neuter Principle

The Christian Scientist's delusion of Christianity is apparent first in its teaching that God is a divine father/mother. This may resonate with the theologically liberal spirit of this age, where some claimants to Christianity believe that God either has a feminine side or actually is female. However, the Christian Scientist's basic concept of God does not fit with the Bible.

God is neither male nor female as we understand gender, yet he reveals himself to us as heavenly Father. Whatever this may mean, and whatever characteristics God may have that seem

---

[12] Attributed to Mark Twain

[13] Leo Rosten, *Religions in America* (New York, Simon and Schuster, 1963) 39.

female to some people, it is not our privilege to change the words of scripture upon a whim.

It turns out, however, that Christian Science doesn't actually think God is both genders, but actually neither one, for its true concept of God is as a principle, like Plato's ideal. Christian Science says God is love, and love is a principle, so God is a principle. It thus confuses the nature of God with one of his attributes.

The Bible consistently describes a personal God, who speaks, commands, works, gives, grieves, sacrifices, pleads, protects, fellowships, plans, knows, and, yes, loves—in short, all the things that we human beings, made in God's image, reflect. In speaking of God in this way, we do not make God like us;[14] we make ourselves like him. This approach is in full accord with what the Bible says about man: "In the image of God created he him."

Jesus Christ—The Best Man

Of the second person of the trinity, God the Son, the Christian Scientist says Jesus is "the highest human expression of the Christ." That definition does not make much sense without knowing how Science redefines the term "Christ" along with dozens of other basic Bible terms.

"Christ," to Christian Science, is a heavenly *idea,* a part of the divine model or reality by which man is to pattern his life. Christ is *not* a person, since God is not personal. Christ is more like a heavenly blueprint, the spirit of perfection and design. Jesus, say Christian Scientists, "is the human man, and Christ is the divine idea; hence the duality of Jesus the Christ."[15]

According to Christian Science, Jesus was not God in the flesh, and cannot be identified exclusively with the Christ. By that theory, anyone could append his name to "Christ"— Joe Christ

---

[14] "Anthropomorphism"

[15] Mary Baker Eddy, *Science and Health with Key to the Scriptures* (Boston, W. F. Brown & Co. Printers, 1875) 473.

and Jane Christ, for example.

Holy Spirit—The Winning Attitude

As for God the Spirit, Christian Science teaches that Jesus, in referring to the coming of a comforter, was speaking of the philosophy, or the "divine science" as they call it, which Christian Science practices. The Christian Scientist holds that his beliefs constitute a spirit or system of knowledge and practice that was foretold as the one who would teach Christians about Christ and remind them of all he had said. In other words, Christian Science itself is the Holy Spirit.

This idea requires a complete redefinition of Bible terms, forcing upon those terms an unnatural sense. Even after Christian Science revises the terms, serious contradictions remain. For instance:

- Peter wrote expressly that the Spirit *speaks.*
- The gospels say that the Spirit *appeared* in bodily form like a dove at the baptism of Jesus.
- Genesis says the Spirit *hovered* over the face of the deep.

This Spirit, as described in the Bible, is no concept or philosophy, no system of beliefs or principles. This Holy Spirit is a personal being, the powerful and active person of the deity himself: this Spirit is God!

Trinity—Three Good Ideas

Based on how the Father, Son and Spirit revealed themselves, orthodox Christianity from the time of the first century developed the inescapable belief that God is one God in three persons. But the nature of the trinity is greatly distorted by the Scientist's concept of God in general and the Spirit as just described. To Christian Science the trinity is "Not three persons in one but as

Life, Truth and Love, or three *offices* of one divine principle."[16]

If this belief were correct, it certainly would mean nothing to be baptized in the personal name of these impersonal, albeit lovely, ideas. Christian Scientists fail to grapple honestly or deeply with the mysterious truths revealed in the Bible concerning the nature of God.

Man—A Shadow Boxer

One of the key concepts that give Christian Science its impetus as a religion of healing is the idea that man is a spiritual reality only, and not a material one; that the flesh is an illusion, that all matter, in fact, is illusion—that it is not real. If this is so, then it would follow that illness is not real, and will disappear if the right thoughts and attitudes are applied to the mind. In essence, man is shadow boxing with illness, and with every human difficulty.

Determining just how far Science wants to go with this idea is difficult, since there are contradictions within its own philosophy. But Mary Eddy went to great lengths in her *Key to the Scriptures* to recast the creation account in Genesis.

According to Eddy's interpretation, God created ideas and heavenly realities; subsequently, a lying tempter and gullible man made up the illusion of the material world. Man, say the Scientists, is an eternal, heavenly reflection of the principle which is God. All the physical side we are acquainted with is a lie. A concept such as this leads to quite a different idea of sin than the one held more typically by Christians.

This is the least of the problems inherent in this concept. If the flesh is an illusion, and what man interprets as illness is illusion, then what he interprets as an experience of wellness should be an illusion as well, should it not? Therefore, what purpose is there in conceptualizing healing? Why should man not simply ignore his experiences entirely and allow his illusory body to die—whatever

---

[16] Duane S. Crowther, *The Godhead* (Horizon Publishers, Springfield, UT, 2008) 36.

that might mean in the context of illusion? Then the illusion would be broken.

In fact, the Christian Scientist does regard death as the liberation of the spiritual person from the illusion of the flesh. So why not encourage death rather than staving it off by seeking to "heal" the "illusions" called diseases? This is the logical conclusion of Christian Science's fundamental assumptions, self-contradictory as they are.

Sin—The Shadow

If flesh is an illusion, what man boxes with is as unreal as he is. For the Scientist, this includes sin; it is an illusion. Mary Eddy wrote, "Man is incapable of sin."[17]

Another church leader says, "Imperfection of every sort belongs to a mortal, material sense of existence... evil is illusory and unreal."[18] This idea stems from the premise that man cannot really act in the material realm, but only in the spiritual realm, and that sin is excluded from that spiritual realm. One noted practitioner wrote, "The false suggestion that evil has an inevitable and overwhelming place in our affairs is basically a lie about God and the universe."[19] The question naturally suggests itself, What should man should call lies, other than sins?

Nevertheless, Scientists say sin is a state of mind. To them it is the belief that there is life apart from God, and they believe that when people wake up from this lie, they will begin to realize their true character as the sinless children of God.

This belief flies in the face of biblical teaching. The Bible says that all have sinned. It says our sins are many, and are as scarlet. It

---

[17] Mary Baker Eddy, *Science and Health with Key to the Scriptures* (Boston, W. F. Brown & Co. Printers, 1875) 475.
[18] Leo Rosten, *What is a Christian Scientist* (New York, Simon and Schuster, 1975) 70.
[19] Leo Rosten, *What is a Christian Scientist* (New York, Simon and Schuster, 1975) 77.

says we are dead in sin until made alive in Christ. These verses and hundreds of others just as plain, are clear statements of divine revelation. When read without mutilating them through fuzzy philosophies forced upon them, their meaning is crystal clear.

The Bible clearly teaches the horrible reality of sin, a spiritual infection that grips humanity, whose character is rebellion against God, self-centeredness and pride, and which leads to a denial of any need for God and his life. It is true there is no life apart from God; but it is possible to *be* apart from God, to be alienated from him, and this distance does not result in "illusion," but in a state of continuing spiritual death—precisely the condition of the sinner. The Christian Scientist exists in just this state—sin—because he denies his guilt and his need of a personal rebirth to life again through the person of Jesus Christ.

Death—The End of Shadows

Mrs. Eddy said, "Man is incapable of death." Christian Science teaches that no one dies; death is not real. The cessation of bodily functions does not constitute death; the spirit is all that matters anyway, and it simply passes over into the realm where there are no more shadows and illusions.

The genuine Christian would agree with Christian Science that the most important thing about this life is its spiritual dimension. But to the Scientist, the thing that we call death just frees everyone to be in a state where there is nothing but bliss and perfection. There is no room in Christian Science for death beyond life, only life beyond life.

Yet the Bible clearly teaches that either is possible. Jesus spoke repeatedly about the two destinations of men, and he reserved eternal life for those who lived and believed in him. But those who refused him while in the flesh would pass over into an everlasting continuation of their "apart-ness from God"—death, in its most emphatic sense.

The result of not believing in the reality of death is that the Christian Scientist does not believe that Jesus actually died.

The result of not believing in the reality of death is that the Christian Scientist does not believe that Jesus actually died. In the words of their philosophy, Jesus was in the tomb demonstrating in the highest sort of way the divine science which he so perfectly reflected. The resurrection was his complete demonstration of the illusory nature of death.

To arrive at this theology, Mary Baker Eddy had to significantly revise and creatively interpret the Bible at dozens of places. For the scripture says Jesus gave up the spirit. Jesus said, "The son of man must be *killed*." He said of Lazarus first that he slept, but then said plainly, "Lazarus is *dead*." Paul said the gospel includes the basic fact that Jesus "*died* for our sins according to the Scriptures." Literally scores of other plain statements of the reality of Jesus' death can be cited. Still, Eddy insisted that both physical life and physical death were illusory.

An illustration from film

Enthusiasts of modern science fiction films may have already recognized a theme in the foregoing description of Christian Science that sounds like the premise of the 1999 film, "The Matrix." This movie "depicts a dystopian future in which humanity is unknowingly trapped inside the Matrix, a simulated reality that intelligent machines have created to distract humans while using their bodies as an energy source."[20] The main character, Neo, is brought to realize that his life in "the world" is really an illusion of sorts, where his thoughts are real but his body and everything else around him are 3D images. The quest of Neo and a few other

---

[20] From "The Matrix," *Wikipedia (https://en.wikipedia.org/ wiki/ The_Matrix #cite_note-Jamie_Allen-8)* Accessed 2023-01-17.

people is to free themselves from this illusory existence.

Critics of Christian Science and of any system of belief that posits that life as we know it is an illusion argue, How can we know, then, that our concept that life as an illusion is not *itself* illusory? How do we know that we are not in an illusion within an illusion? A dream within a dream? The reader can see that once begun, the idea that we are in some sort of realistic dream might be circular and have no end.

In reference to the Christian Scientist's concept of Christ's death having been an illusion, it takes incredible mental and grammatical gymnastics to make anything of all this but that Jesus really died, and that his actual, physical death accomplished something for us in the way of payment for our sin. These gymnastics are supplied in the textbook for Christian Science: *Science and Health With Key to the Scriptures.* The claims for this book would, if true, make it something astronomically more significant than any commentary or volume on theology ever written by any orthodox Christian as a help to understanding the Bible. To the Scientist, the Bible is incomplete as written: it needs something else to complete it and make it clear.

Revelation—The Bible Needs Something

Mary Baker's philosophizing on her experience resulted in her book, *Science and Health*. Through the tunnel-vision she imposed on herself by her obsession with mental healing, and partly owing to her negative reactions to staunch Calvinism, she forced scripture into an interpretive mold it does not fit. And her writings, principally *Science and Health with Key to the Scriptures,* are accorded by her followers a status nearly (if not fully) equal to the Bible itself.

One spokesman-practitioner said of Mrs. Eddy that she is "*the* revelator to this age,"[21] and Mrs. Eddy says of her own writing that

---

[21] *The Christian Science Journal* (New York, Christian Science Publishing Society, 1906) 62.

it is "by the revelation of Jesus Christ."[22] In Sunday services in a Christian Science church, one sees two lecterns, or reading desks, identically designed and equally placed in the room, upon which sit the Bible and *Science and Health,* respectively. During the service, portions are read from each, equally, and given the same weight. Scientists are encouraged to study Eddy's writings as they would study the Bible.

The Bible itself prophesies the coming of philosophies that distort the plain truth of God (2 Cor. 4:2). Rewriting or remolding the concepts of the scripture is a direct violation of the commandments of Jesus Christ (Rev. 22:18-19). And the Bible applies the term "antichrist" to anyone who denies that Jesus Christ is come in the flesh—which means he had real, human existence (I John 4:1-4).

The spirit of antichrist, said John, is already in the world. Judged on the basis of Christian Science's own statement of doctrines, the spirit of antichrist is quite active in their teachings.

Salvation—Waking Up from the Dream

If sin and death do not exist, logically no need for salvation from them exists, either; but Christian Science also redefines salvation. It means to wake up from the dream of mortality, of life without God. When you take up Christian Science, their practitioners would claim, you experience this awakening and begin to enjoy the benefits of spiritual life, through the science of Christ.

The Delusion of Being Scientific

Science for the Christian Scientist, as we have already seen, does not mean biochemical and physical research and testing, but quite the opposite. "Science" means knowledge; the Christian

---

[22] Ibid, 107.

Scientists' science claims to be the knowledge of Christ, or the acceptance and practice of the divine pattern for life.

Most important to this science, as we have seen, is the denial of the reality of the physical world. The most focused-on consequence of this premise for the Christian Scientist is the matter of health and healing. If matter is not real, sickness is not real, and its negative effect on us can be dispelled by the proper attitudes. Mrs. Eddy made her motto, "The truth will make you free."

One Christian Science writer summarized the religion's belief in this way: "As the individual understands his true selfhood to be spiritual rather than material, he is able to follow the example of Jesus Christ in overcoming the ills and evils of the flesh. This is the process described by St. Paul as putting off the old man and putting on the new... Health is a spiritual reality, not a physical condition... The object of Christian Science is not primarily to heal physical disease but to regenerate human thought and character. Healing is the effect of attaining this spiritual regeneration in some degree."[23]

A fragment of truth is in these ideas. Their partial truth is what makes them believable. But the error outweighs any truth in them. What confuses people is the persistent claim, with some semblance of proof, that this "science" works. Libraries hold books of testimonies by persons who claim to have been healed of all sorts of diseases through the application of the principles of Christian Science, and without medicines or treatment by doctors. What about such claims?

First of all, Matthew 7:22 says, "Many will say to me on that day, 'Lord, Lord, did we not... drive out demons and perform many miracles?'" The occurrence of a wonder does not prove the activity of God. It may as easily prove the activity of Satan. In addition to that, it can be noted that a vast number of healings

---

[23] Rosten, op. cit., 70.

from Christian Science are for conditions that frequently do, or theoretically can, result from psychosomatic causes. Christian Scientists claim, however, that in many cases bone fractures are set and healed under Christian Science treatment. But officially, "Science and Health makes provision for a Christian Scientist to employ a surgeon to set a bone if the Christian Scientist has not reached the degree of understanding needed for healing by spiritual means alone."[24]

Such concessions and compromises suggest the conclusion that Christian Science is hedging and rationalizing. After all, if flesh is illusory, and sickness, too, then what about poverty and hunger, both complications of fleshly life? Mrs. Eddy admitted they also were illusory, and she presumed that Christian Science would someday be able to counteract them. She asserted, however, that "in the present stage of our understanding of the Science, we can only demonstrate against sickness, and not against hunger and money."[25] Her admission is convenient. There is no psychosomatic poverty. And Christian Science, on its way to being two centuries old, still hasn't arrived at that state of its art, and it never will.

The fundamental assumption of Scientists about the illusory nature of the physical world strongly suggests a problem with logic: If the flesh is not real, why do Christian Scientists care at all about healing it—or concerning themselves with it in any way? If matter is a dream, and there is nothing to be saved from and no one to save, why not be happy hedonists or apathetic atheists? The philosophy of Christian Science, however, is too heavy with internal contradiction to allow logic to prevail.

Reject Science: Seek Truth

This brief survey of Christian Science allows us to draw some

---

[24] Rosten, op. cit., 77.
[25] John H. Gerstner, *The Teachings of Christian Science* (Grand Rapids, Baker Book House, 1975) 17.

conclusions, which can operate as guidelines for the true Christian in his thought and possible witness.

Foremost among these guiding thoughts is that Christian Science has all the typical earmarks of a cult:

- A central figure other than Jesus Christ revered to excess;
- A writing placed alongside the Bible and considered in practice as of equal importance with the word of God;
- Significant redefinition of basic Bible concepts and terms, upon a foundation of one person's experience and interpretation; and
- Appeal to the common human desire to avoid personal repentance from sin and confession of the need of salvation through a new birth.

Tips for conversation with a Christian Scientist

- *Scriptures.* A Christian who believes he may have opportunity to converse with a Christian Scientist and possibly to share the gospel should certainly be aware of scriptures that firmly oppose these ideas, like some of those we have referenced or quoted above.
- *Reasonable argument.* As well, some of the logical arguments we have made here might be of use, especially with someone who may already be struggling with his or her beliefs.
- *Gospel.* Above all, the Christian's thorough knowledge of the Biblical gospel of Jesus Christ, and an ability to find and use the various Bible passages explaining the plan of salvation, is imperative. The Bible says that the gospel itself is "the power of God unto salvation" (Romans 1:16). When the word of God is employed, the Spirit of God works!

How tragic to realize that many people have passed from this flesh into the presence of God who have claimed to have followed the way of truth, but to whom Christ Jesus has now said, "I never knew you." The basis of judgment will not be how many diseases one is healed of, physically or mentally, or how many miracles one either experiences or performs, or in fact any other claim to great deeds. Judgment will be based on each person's having a relationship with the living and personal God through his one and only Son and Christ, Jesus, who died for sin on the cross, and who was raised from the grave. He lives, at the right hand of the throne of God and imparts life through his Spirit to all who will receive him as Lord.

No "science" or technique is required to experience deliverance from sin and the gift of eternal life. Salvation requires only confession of sin and then turning from sin and self to Jesus. Receiving him in surrender as Lord results in everlasting life, a life that begins now, in this flesh—a very real experience with the Holy Spirit—and then continues into eternity in the presence of God.

Humanism
The Ultimate Unbelief
(Romans 1:18-32)

A story goes that a little fish was swimming with a school of friends one day, when he spotted a larger fish about to prey on the stragglers of their group. He darted madly about, warning the other fish, who quickly turned and got away; only one or two became dinner for the preying fish. A while later, another fish of a different variety, larger than the last, spotted them, and came their way. Again the fish scurried about, regrouped above and beyond the enemy, and got away. By this time they were feeling proud they had eluded these would-be captors.

The day went that way, with only a few little fish lost to the many species of predators that would make them into a quick meal. They were proud, their leaders were proud, as they swam in the beauty of the deep ocean. They were still feeling satisfied with their success at eluding their enemies when the night fell a little too suddenly, and closed like doors in front of the whole school, and all was dark. They slid together down a long passageway to oblivion, and the whale glided silently away.

Since the early 1960s, when a surge in cults began, most genuinely Christian groups have been taking some steps to warn believers away from cults and variant religions. This little book seeks to accomplish that goal. The rash of eastern myths and modern constructs has been so obvious and so scary that Christians who jealously guard their biblical beliefs could not have missed the many dangers surrounded them. But Christians may be successful in avoiding cults and defending their flocks well against their false teachings, only to suddenly be gulped down by the greatest religious enemy of all: Humanism.

Humanism is the ultimate unbelief. There is no greater philosophical enemy to genuine Christian faith than humanism. One major daily newspaper recently carried some debate on its editorial pages as to what humanism is. One editor, joined by an elderly minister, said it was just an admirable attitude and philosophy of life which encouraged benevolence and progress. But person after person wrote in to say that humanism is a menace to man, because it denies the reality of God, and denies man's need for him.

A common dictionary definition for humanism is helpful:

Humanism… any system of thought or action based on the nature, dignity, interests, and ideals of man; specif., a modern, non-theistic, rationalist movement that holds that man is capable of self-fulfillment, ethical conduct, etc. without recourse to supernaturalism.[26]

Virtually synonymous with humanism is the term secularism, which means "a system of doctrines and practices that disregards or rejects any form of religious faith and worship."[27]

Sometimes humanism is called "Religious Humanism," due to the fact that it is commonly classified as a religious faith. More often, it is known as "secular humanism," and the Supreme Court of the United States has called it a religion in various decisions.[28] For all the warnings issued by pastors, churches and denominations, however, sometimes Christians miss humanism's points of impact on their lives. If evangelical Christians are to fend off the insidious destruction of secular humanism, they must

---

[26] *Webster's New World Dictionary,* Second College Edition (1980), s.v. "humanism."

[27] Ibid., s.v. "secularism."

[28] In Torcaso v. Watkins, 1961, the U. S. Supreme Court held: "We repeat and again reaffirm that neither a State nor the Federal Government can constitutionally force a person 'to profess a belief or disbelief in any religion.'" In explanation of the paragraph including the previous statement, footnote 11 of the Court's decision said further: "Among religions in this country which do not teach what would generally be considered a belief in the existence of God are Buddhism, Taoism, Ethical Culture, Secular Humanism and others."

In the 1963 case of Abington vs Schempp, the Court held that "the State may not establish a "religion of secularism" in the sense of affirmatively opposing or showing hostility to religion, thus "preferring those who believe in no religion over those who do believe."

identify this menace to man.

The apostle Paul addressed the Roman Christians about a similar movement in his own day. In his letter to the Roman Christians, Paul identified the root philosophy that produces all sorts of licentiousness and perversion. What he described is humanism, as it was reflected in the mind of the first century pagan.

> **The wrath of God is being revealed from heaven against all the godlessness and wickedness of men who suppress the truth by their wickedness, since what may be known about God is plain to them, because God has made it plain to them. For since the creation of the world God's invisible qualities—his eternal power and divine nature—have been clearly seen, being understood from what has been made, so that men are without excuse. For although they knew God, they neither glorified him as God nor gave thanks to him, but their thinking became futile and their foolish hearts were darkened...They exchanged the truth of God for a lie, and worshiped and served created things rather than the Creator...Because of this, God gave them over to shameful lusts. Even their women exchanged natural relations for unnatural ones. In the same way the men also abandoned natural relations with women and were inflamed with lust for one another... Furthermore, since they did not think it worthwhile to retain the knowledge of God, he gave them over to a depraved mind...They have become filled with every kind of wickedness...they invent ways of doing evil... Although they know God's righteous decree that those who do such things deserve death, they not only continue to do these very things but also approve of those who practice them (Romans 1:18ff).**

In these verses, Paul delivered what was one of his most extensive and impassioned warnings, against an approach to life that many people adopt to this very day, and which is more menacing to the health of society and the development of faith in God than any other form of disbelief. Humanism is that approach, and it wears many faces.

As a means to aid in recognition and then defense, consider five distinctive things that humanism is.

A Document Placed Ominously at the Heart of a Movement

A congress of humanists in 1933 gave birth to a document called the Humanist Manifesto, which served as the doctrinal basis for the rapidly growing movement of humanism and secularism in Western countries. Again in 1973, a humanist congress composed and signed the Humanist Manifesto II, restating and updating the original document. While the number of persons actually responsible for the origination of the document is relatively small, its impact is spreading like ripples in a pool. Over forty percent of U.S. Congressmen and many top educators at the time signed the Humanist Manifesto II. Not everyone knows of the document itself, but the ideas expressed in it are widely known, and increasingly believed. What are some of the things it declares as humanist doctrines?

It says:

Religious humanists regard the universe as self-existing and not created…Man is a part of nature and…has emerged as the result of a continuous process…Humanism asserts that the nature of the universe depicted by modern science makes unacceptable any supernatural or cosmic guarantees of human values…

It also says:

> We find insufficient evidence for belief in the existence of a supernatural; it is either meaningless or irrelevant to the question of the survival and fulfillment of the human…No deity will save us; we must save ourselves… Promises of immortal salvation or fear of eternal damnation are both illusory and harmful.

Based on this kind of belief, the Humanist Manifesto II puts forward these behavioral goals:

> We affirm that moral values derive their source from human experience. Ethics is autonomous and situational, needing no theological or ideological sanction…we strive for the good life, here and now… We believe that intolerant attitudes often cultivated by orthodox religions…unduly repress sexual conduct. The right to birth control, abortion, and divorce should be recognized… The many varieties of sexual exploration should not in themselves be considered evil.

Additionally, the second Manifesto supports the ideas of euthanasia (mercy killing), and suicide, and encourages the development of programs that will put children under government supervision at an early age, and that will discourage the development and maintenance of families.

On the political level, it declares the elimination of separate nations and the formation of one-world government to be the goal, with a socialistic order to be preferred.

At the turn of the Millennium, Paul Kurtz, editor of the *Free Inquiry*, drafted the Humanist Manifesto 2000. Among its more than fifty signers were many university professors in the U. S. And

Great Britain.[29] The document was more moderate in tone than the 1973 Manifesto, but it continued its invectives against religion, particularly Christianity. In the section on Religious Skepticism, the document states: "[Secular humanists] reject the idea that God has intervened miraculously in history or revealed himself to a chosen few or that he can save or redeem sinners... We reject the divinity of Jesus..."[30]

While only a few persons have actually signed the various humanist manifestos, the whole movement is characterized by the things these documents verbalize.

The importance of these humanist documents in the humanist movement should not be understated. While only a few persons have actually signed the various humanist manifestos, the whole movement is characterized by the things these documents verbalize. Few people signed the Declaration of Independence, but millions of Americans subscribe to the convictions it expresses.

At least in part, humanism is a document or documents standing at the heart of a movement—documents that deny the key concepts and teachings of the Bible, which Christians believe God inspired so as to reveal himself to man.

- The Bible begins with the assumption of God, and predicates all morality and purpose in life upon that reality. Humanism begins with the presumption there is no God, and bases its

---

[29] The Humanist Manifesto 2000, like the Humanist Manifesto II, carries the endorsements of Isaac Asimov, who died in 1992, and B. F. Skinner, who died in 1990.

[30] In addition to its denial of the divinity of Jesus, the Humanist Manifesto states its signers' opposition to the right of parents to bring up their children in their faith: "Although children should learn about the history of religious moral practices, these young minds should not be indoctrinated in a faith before they are mature enough to evaluate the merits for themselves."

recommended "morality" on the consequent absence of absolute standards. In fact, the *Humanist Manifesto II* bluntly says that morals and ethics are "situational."[31]

- The Bible says man's purpose here is to live in fellowship with God and to serve him. Humanism declares man should live for himself and should imagine no higher being to whom to be loyal.
- The Bible says that although God has made an ordered, scientific world, he has often broken into history through strategic catastrophe and exceptional events—commonly called miracles. Humanism denies that supernatural events take place, since there is no supernatural being.
- The Bible says the reality of God is plain enough—even obvious, and that the God reflected in creation is to be worshiped. Humanists, however, deify man and exalt him.

Humanism is not merely an impersonal document, however, as if a religion or philosophy could exist without people being proponents of it. Its vast ranks are represented by many leaders in government, academia, and other professions.

A Cadre of Leaders in Various Fields

The authors of the Humanist Manifestos constitute an organization of humanists dedicated to their cause. The American Humanist Association, which publishes "The Humanist" magazine, unites leaders from various professional fields and vocations into a body, planning for the success of the humanist movement. Many prominent persons throughout society are

---

[31] "We affirm that moral values derive their source from human experience. Ethics is autonomous and situational, needing not theological or ideological sanction. Ethics stems from human need and interest." —*Humanist Manifesto II*

humanists and represent well the key concepts of the movement. Well-known advocates of humanistic philosophy include Isaac Asimov in literature and popular-science, Carl Sagan in physics and astronomy, Sigmund Freud and B. F. Skinner in Psychology, John Dewey in education, Ben Bova in publishing, Richard Dawkins in evolutionary biology, and hosts of others (at this writing, only Dawkins is still living).

Humanist leaders appear to possess an unseen bond and to be guided by a very personal, unseen force.

Not every public figure operating on humanistic principles says, "I am a humanist." Many humanists characterize themselves by their backgrounds or politics and avoid terminology that might make them unpopular with some people. Others candidly declare themselves humanists and preach their philosophy with conviction. Whether avowed or not, these humanists in various fields affect people's lives in sometimes profound ways.

An amazing unity of anti-theistic thought exists among even unorganized humanists throughout society. The Christian who is sensitive to the reality of spiritual powers in the world today may recognize an other-worldly element in the humanist movement. Humanist leaders appear to possess an unseen bond and to be guided by a very personal, unseen force.

One of the early humanists of modern times was Charles Darwin. Christians since the early part of the twentieth century have voiced continuing objection to Darwin's theory of evolution, and have thought that the most significant problem with the theory was Darwin's opinion of how life came about. Meanwhile, believers have all too often ignored the most damaging element of Darwin's beliefs—his philosophy that there is no God responsible for the universe and what is in it. Unfortunately, Darwin's ideas were prominent among atheists of his day who urged him to publish his work, and humanists since Darwin's day have revered

The Origin of Species as one of the core documents of secular humanism.

The theory of evolution is crucial to the humanist movement. It is a central doctrine, upon which most of the rest of humanist beliefs rest either in part or in whole. Because evolution is so critical to the humanist world view, Christians should be alert to the temptation to blend its concepts with the Bible.

For instance, the heart of evolution as a biological concept is that, beginning with single-cell organisms, one species evolved into another, resulting eventually in all living things in the world today including human beings. The Bible, however—whether read from a literal or figurative point of view, represents the creation of different kinds of animals in a distinct fashion, and carefully says that God made man specially, at a particular point in time, and gave him a spirit or soul. Blending these two viewpoints, evolutionary and biblical, into what is often called "theistic evolution" cannot be done without eroding confidence in the biblical witness. Furthermore, accepting the proposition that man evolved from lower forms of life lays a faulty foundation for the interpretation of the rest of the Bible. Key Bible concepts of the nature of man and the presence of sin in the world are totally undone by denying that God made an actual Adam and Eve as the first two human beings, from whom the entire human race descended.

The theory of evolution is just one of the many humanistic ideas that have attained almost official status in this country and in much of the world. This fact points up another facet to the identity of humanism.

A National Policy Reflected in Numerous Institutions

The federal government is involved in promulgating humanist values through legislation that increasingly threatens the liberties of Christians and churches, by subjecting them to tax intrusion, coercing them to change their values, restricting their witness or influence, and generally harassing them. The federal government and most state governments reflect humanistic values in many policies. The chief institution representing and promoting humanism, however, is the public school system. As innocent as some public school teachers are, tragically the system is overwhelmingly biased toward secular humanism. The influence of John Dewey, the father of modern public education, over the philosophy by which schools operate today, has resulted in schooling that is more and more at odds with religious values—especially Christian ones.

The chief institution representing and promoting humanism is the public school system.

Are these statements excessive exaggerations? Listen to what "The Humanist" magazine said in Jan-Feb 1983: "The battle for mankind's future must be waged and won in the public school classroom by teachers who correctly perceive their role as the proselytizer of a new faith—a religion of humanity... utilizing a classroom instead of a pulpit to convey humanist values in whatever subject they teach."[32] The late Dr. Frances Schaeffer, who stirred the world of Christians with his thought-provoking analysis of the condition of our faith, said, "Law and government are used by humanism as a tool to force this false view and its results on everyone."[33] Ben Fisher, for eight years the executive secretary of the Southern Baptist Education Commission, said in a speech to the Association of Southern Baptist Colleges and Schools, that the public school system "has become another tremendous influence negating Christian values and belief in the

---

[32] "The Humanist," Jan-Feb 1983.
[33] Frances Schaeffer, *How Then Shall We Live* (Grand Rapids, Fleming H. Revell Co, 1976) 154.

supernatural, not so much from open assault as from the insidious and persistent ignoring of religious values from kindergarten through university."[34]

Things are worse some places than others, and every exception to this worsening pattern is cause for thanksgiving and excitement. But Christian teachers know best of all that the situation is becoming bleak in public education. And since the school injects persons into every walk of society, the trend of humanism and secularism in education has resulted in the rise of a whole generation of secularists. Thus, humanism is not only a policy in public institutions, but it is a pervasive, secular "faith."

A Religion of Secularism Pervading the Society

The average person not formally involved in a religion or reared in a religious family has simply been trained to ignore religion, ignore God, ignore the Bible, and occupy his life with anything and everything else. The chief reason he is able to do this without feeling the part of the rebel is that he has been thoroughly indoctrinated with the notion that he is just a well-groomed secular animal, content with attaining earthly desires and gratifying material wants.

The humanist discards religious claims and makes the assumption he has no soul. He anticipates no eternity, and believes he has no responsibility to a holy God. Harvey Cox, author of *The Secular City,* wrote in 1965 this up-to-date description of humanism: "The forces of secularization have no serious interest in persecuting religion. Secularization simply bypasses and undercuts religion and goes on to other things. It has relativized religious world-views and thus rendered them innocuous."[35]

---

[34] In a speech
[35] Harvey Cox, *The Secular City* (New York, Macmillan Publishing, 1990) 2.

Jimmy Absalom has written that this kind of secular mind set, which permeates every area of study and every institution of society, "is the most devastating and most subtle of ideologies opposed to Christianity that has ever emerged, including Communism." Paul's description was particularly apt of humanists today: "They did not think it worthwhile to retain the knowledge of God."

Helping to perpetuate this method of life that pays no serious attention to religion is a media establishment dominated by secularists. Interviews with 240 top writers and broadcasters a few years ago showed that fifty percent reject any religious affiliation. Only eight percent went to church or synagogue regularly, and eighty-six percent never attended religious services. Fifty-four percent considered themselves left of center politically, and only nineteen percent on the right. Over ninety percent of media elite support abortion on demand, and seventy-five percent are in favor of so-called "homosexual rights." And they are virtually unanimous in their support of what is called sexual expression and freedom, which means unmarried and extramarital sexual relations.[36] Most of the foregoing statistics have become even more antithetical to Christianity (or even Judaism) in the succeeding years.

This moral license is exactly what God says characterizes societies and peoples who abandon his purpose for them. The Holy Spirit tells us through Paul what is happening in our own day as well as what happened in his: "God gave them over in the sinful desires of their hearts to sexual impurity for the degrading of their bodies with one another" (Romans 1:28). Homosexuality, lesbianism, transgenderism, and marital unfaithfulness of every kind, as well as rampant abortion, the sharp rise of venereal diseases, and abandonment of family solidarity and permanence, are all reflections of the anchor-less heart of man under humanism.

---

[36] Fred Barnes, "Can We Trust the News?" *Reader's Digest,* Jan. 1988, 37-38.

The humanist intended to turn the world into paradise by his own hand, unaided by a God he thought did not exist. But it is fast becoming hell on earth; and surely the God who does in fact live and reign on high will not wait much longer to relieve his people by way of judgment. The greatest reason he will judge is not the mess we are in, (which is a kind of judgment in itself), but the extreme iniquity of this humanism that is currently driving culture to its doom.

An Elevation of Pride to its Ultimate Form

The original sin, pride, has been made into a religion. The first sinful thought, that man could determine his own course of behavior without reference to the revealed will of God, is now a full-blown religion, with a creed, a set of scriptures, a loose-knit priesthood, and of course its deity, man himself, in all his collective, self-perceived glory. Many Baals have been cast down by God, and many idol worshipers have been judged through conquering armies, internal disintegration, and gradual demise. But man's undisguised, unashamed worship of himself takes us back to the sin of Babel, where men united to do whatever their hearts desired, believing such to be the only value of life. Such self-worship takes us back to the days of Noah, when according to God's word, "The Lord saw how great man's wickedness on the earth had become, and that every inclination of the thoughts of his heart was only evil all the time" (Genesis 6:5 NIV). God's response to this situation was unwaveringly final.

This is a time for awareness and wariness, for not only Evangelicals but true Christians of all denominational families. Believers need to be aware of what humanism is in order to recognize it in street clothes—because that is the only garb it dons. And Christians need to be wary of humanism's many subtle ways of infecting thought and life. Every Christian probably could make a long list of things that reveal how humanist philosophy has invaded his or her opinions and habits.

One typical way in which Christians practice humanism is by sectioning off part of their lives to devote to religion, while failing to relate Christian faith at all to the rest of their lives. Thus, most of their lives are secular, and only a small part sacred. But God has made all of life sacred, and designed none of it to be restrictively secular. All of life is to have the stamp of God's will and approval on it.

Believers need to be aware of what humanism is in order to recognize it in street clothes—because that is the only garb it dons.

There is no area of creation on which God's claim does not fall. The world is not the accident of evolution, but rather the creation of God. He involves himself intimately in it, and holds man, who is his highest creation, responsible for living in conformity with his divine will. Before any and all other goals, the follower of Christ is to submit to the will of the living God!

Talking to humanist friends

A humanist may not identify himself or herself as such, and may be unaware that humanism is the "religion" he adheres to. But even if he does:

- *Bible discussion.* The Christian witness should identify specific humanist "doctrines" and rely on the Bible to counter them. Remember that humanism tends to be a blanket denial of Bible truths. The Christian will generally not be able to "prove" the Bible to the humanist, but he must rely on the word of God to exercise its own power.
- *Calm and reasonable.* Avoid mere argument. While a logical "argument" may be employed, a heated disagreement will certainly be ineffective and may destroy further opportunities to witness.

- *Pray.* Bathe any attempt at witness in prayer—before, during and after any conversation.
- *Patience.* Try thinking of witness to a humanist acquaintance as a long-term series of short encounters, including casual, personal testimony to how God has blessed and worked in your life.

Paul wrote, "Although they claimed to be wise, they became fools" (Rom.1:22). The Bible says, "The fool has said in his heart there is no God" (Proverbs 14:1). May God grant his people the strength of his Spirit to remain wise, by continuing to reverence and obey him; and may he help Christians to instruct this foolish world in the way of wisdom, that many who now virtually worship the created thing might turn to "worship the Creator, who is forever praised—Amen!" (Romans 1:25).

Islam
Religion a la Allah
(Hebrews 1:1-3,2:9,3:1-3)

Academic approaches to religion usually speak broadly of the three great monotheistic faiths of the world: Judaism, Christianity, and Islam. For the Christian, the study of new or extreme cult groups leads much more easily to a clear understanding of their fallacies than does a study of one of the "big three."

Most Christians would find it easier to present the gospel to a member of the Hare Krishna sect than to a Jew or a Muslim. In fact, some people who are nominally involved in the Christian faith, while they might generally believe in the New Testament doctrine of salvation through belief in Jesus, tend to make exceptions for Jews and Muslims on grounds that they "all worship the same God." It is particularly troubling that some statements have come out of Catholic sources supporting the idea that Jews can be eternally saved without obeying the gospel of Christ.[37] Something about Judaism, Christianity and Islam results in their being considered as all having a path to heaven, by most everyone except devoted Jews, Christians, and Muslims!

The something they have in common is a their faith-history, at least in the very early stages. The Old Testament is accepted by all three in some way. To Jews, the books of Genesis through Malachi are the complete scriptures, referred to by them sometimes as the *Tanakh*. To Christians, these books are the Old Testament (or "Covenant"), which, with the New Testament, become the complete Bible. Muslims add the Qu'ran and call it complete, though they believe the Old Testament is corrupted. The interpretation of various Old Testament teachings differs among Jews, Christians and Muslims, of course. Nevertheless, a certain

---

[37] Stoyan Zaimov, "Jews Are Saved Even Without Believing in Christ, Vatican Claims," The Christian Post, October 18, 2023, https://www.christianpost.com/news/jews-saved-heaven-salvation-without-jesus-christ-vatican-claims-pope-francis-israel.html.

bulk of history, and some cardinal truths, are common to the three.

But commonality does not mean shared destiny. Christians believe devotedly the words of Jesus: "I am the way, the truth and the life. No man comes unto the Father but by me." In the unique life, death and resurrection of Jesus Christ Christians find unsurpassed authority and are convinced that all persons must seek a saving relationship with God through him, or they are destined to die in sin and be forever separated from God.

If we truly believe that, we cannot exclude witness to a Jew or a Muslim, for neither believes in the uniqueness of Jesus Christ and the necessity of proclaiming him exclusive Lord and Savior.

Islam is the most recent on the scene of the three major monotheistic religions. In a world where the Islamic culture has thrust itself upon the world stage in the most dramatic way, the Christian will care enough to know about Islam, so that he can find inroads to share his faith effectively, should the opportunity arise.

A good starting point is the perspective of history offered by the author of Hebrews, who wrote:

In the past God spoke to our ancestors through the prophets at many times and in various ways, but in these last days he has spoken to us by his Son, whom he appointed heir of all things, and through whom also he made the universe. The Son is the radiance of God's glory and the exact representation of his being, sustaining all things by his powerful word. After he had provided purification for sins, he sat down at the right hand of the Majesty in heaven(Hebrews 1:1-3 NIV).

…But we do see Jesus, who was made lower than the angels for a little while, now crowned with glory and honor because he suffered death, so that by the grace of God he might taste death for everyone.

(Hebrews 2:9 NIV).

Therefore, holy brothers and sisters, who share in the heavenly calling, fix your thoughts on Jesus, whom we acknowledge as our apostle and high priest. He was faithful to the one who appointed him, just as Moses was faithful in all God's house. Jesus has been found worthy of greater honor than Moses, just as the builder of a house has greater honor than the house itself. For every house is built by someone, but God is the builder of everything. "Moses was faithful as a servant in all God's house," bearing witness to what would be spoken by God in the future. But Christ is faithful as the Son over God's house. And we are his house, if indeed we hold firmly to our confidence and the hope in which we glory (3:1-6, NIV).

One of the Holy Spirit's miracles in us is that he can cause us to be fearless in truth while still being loving in grace. We need that approach with Muslim friends, for Islam is a way of life that denies the only Saviorhood and Sonship of Jesus Christ.

The Roots of Islam

Islam has its roots in the Arab world.[38] The religion began in the seventh century, but its roots go back to Abraham, and before him to Adam; for the Islamic faith is tied uniquely to the Arabs, who come from Adam through Shem, to Abraham, just as the Jews. But their family tree goes not through Isaac, son of Abraham with Sarah, but through Ishmael, borne by Haggar, the handmaiden.

---

[38] The term "Arab" technically refers to inhabitants of the Middle East or North Africa who speak Arabic. However, it is often used in connection to inhabitants of a wider region. In this work we use "Arab" loosely to refer to Semitic non-Jews whether or not Arabic speaking.

Genesis says Ishmael and his descendants settled in the deserts and lived in hostility toward their brethren, the descendants of Isaac. So it has been down through the centuries. Throughout the period reflected in the Old Testament, no peoples were more subject to isolation, skirmishing, and shifting alliances than the Arabs. They lived in difficult terrains and climes and owed allegiance to few outside their families, as they pursued their nomadic existence. Along the way, the idols of the farther eastern countries, the Babylonians and Assyrians, accumulated in their sparse culture. This was the character of the Arab world through the sixth century A.D. Then something happened that began to change that character radically.

The Birth of Islam

A man named Mohammed was born in 571 in Mecca, in Saudi Arabia. A man of gentle disposition in a world of hostility, Mohammed was an introvert and a brooding dreamer. He spent long periods of time in the hills outside Mecca, especially Mt. Hira, where in solitude he reckoned with his own life, speculated about the desert jinn (the demons thought to inhabit the land) and about the one god thought to be greater than all of the others, Allah. He also thought on the great need of Arab people to find unity and national direction.

Islam set out from the first to contradict and deny every major tenet of Judaism and Christianity.

Although Mohammed was basically unschooled, he was not entirely ignorant of the history of Semitic peoples, including the Jews. He knew the basics of Old Testament and New Testament events, and the importance of figures such as Abraham, Moses, and Jesus. But in the desert during his young years, a rearrangement and transformation of these things took place in his mind.

At the same time he began to see himself as a mystic and a prophet—perhaps, he thought, like the prophets of old. It is unlikely that anything strictly analytical went on in his mind during that metamorphosis-like process, but somehow the need of the Arab people blended together with his emerging self-image. He came up with a belief that was then unconventional for Arabs: "There is no god but Allah!"

This Allah, he said, was the God of Jewish history, who spoke through Abraham, Moses, and others; and, he was the God who sent Jesus, whom Mohammed believed to be a great prophet. This new faith, which demands the surrender of a person to a belief in, and to the doing of the will of, the one god, Allah, is called Islam, which means surrender.

As Mohammed began to return to his society with this conviction and experienced its hostility to his ideas, he began to believe that he was called to be a prophet of Allah, like Moses and Jesus before him. Continuing to retreat to the desert in typical prophet fashion, he began to scrawl on bones and skins what he thought to be revealed prophecies.

He gained a small following in Mecca, but rejection was the rule. However, in nearby Medina acceptance was far greater, and he and his followers took flight there in A.D. 622. The move was significant, for he became an administrator, a power broker, and an instant leader. And he began to plan the unification of Arab peoples. Under Mohammed, believers in Islam penetrated the whole Arab world, and much of the Mediterranean countries, and they used not only persuasion but force as well, to convert non-believers.

Mohammed died as any other man, and although there are traditions that say that he ascended miraculously, the claim is not cardinal to Islam, because Islam does not regard Mohammed as anything more than a prophet. The great confession of Islam is, "There is but one God—Allah, and Mohammed is his prophet."

Nevertheless, Islam would not exist without this man and what he wrote down. The whole faith and its notable flaws trace to him.

From Mohammed and his teachings come Islam, and the teachings outline what are known as the five pillars of Islam.

The Pillars of Islam

God, Mohammed, and the Qur'an

The first pillar is really three things: God, Mohammed, and the Qur'an. Islam holds to a radical monotheism not unlike that of Judaism, except that Muslims seem to be more excessive in their stress of this characteristic of God. Islam arose in a polytheistic culture; so it is not surprising to find it placing a premium on Allah's unique standing. But Islam seems angry about its monotheism. This is not surprising, however, since Allah is an angry God.

Though many of their scriptures describe Allah as peaceful and gracious, many more characterize him as wrathful, vengeful and harsh; and the general temper of Islam reflects belief in a God whose gentleness takes the back seat to his justice—the reverse of the Christian understanding of the LORD.

The New Testament as we know it, building on the Old, reveals a God who is just and holy, but whose grace and love are his own preferred motivations. He had rather redeem than get revenge (see 2 Peter 3:9). Yet, for Mohammed, Allah's demands outweighed his grace; and Mohammed's personal experience is crucial to Islam.

Islam refers to Mohammed as the "Seal of the Prophets," meaning the last and greatest of the prophets, which include the great prophetic figures of the Bible. Muslims regard Jesus not as the incarnate God the Son, but only as the greatest of prophets up unto to his time; however, they regard Mohammed as having received the fullest revelation of eternal truths.

Some nominal Christians might not object to conceding that Mohammed may be a prophet, but orthodox Jews and Biblical Christians must beg to differ. Working from a belief in the authority of the Old and New Testaments, several conditions inhere in prophecy:

- First, the prophet must be sent. In most cases, this is known only by the testimony of the prophet himself, and by the evidential nature of his message and work.
- Second is the "prophet's" message and work itself. It must conform to the revelation of God that has been received and verified before it. It must confirm, not deny, what God has said at other times.
- In consequence, the Christian cannot accept the claim to prophecy that Mohammed made because in it he assumes a place above Christ and denies his eternal Sonship and redemptive work.

It is interesting that Muslims accept the virgin birth of Christ and a number of other things concerning him. They even believe he will return at the last day. But they refuse to accept the New Testament word concerning him, and his own testimony recorded there: "I and the Father are one… Before Abraham was, I am… He that has seen me has seen the Father." And our focal text above clearly says that God has "appointed [Christ] heir of all things," and that through Christ God "made the universe." The passage claims that the Son, Jesus Christ, is "the exact representation of [God's] being." These claims identify Jesus Christ as God the Son Incarnate.

Islam denies all this. This is only one problem with the teachings of Mohammed, which are part of the third item in the first pillar of Islam.

The teachings of Islam are communicated in the Qur'an, a book put together from the writings of Mohammed, which he claimed were direct revelations from Allah. Orthodox Muslims claim that the book was dictated in the order found in the Qur'an today, by the angel Gabriel, and that Mohammed simply transcribed them.

The historical facts, however, indicate otherwise. The writing took place over a period of some twenty-three years and history is fairly clear that upon Mohammed's death there was no neat package of his writings. The leaders and successors of the faith gathered the various fragments of his teachings and arranged them into the present order. There has never been any revision, for Muslims uniformly regard the Qur'an as perfect in every way.

The Qur'an's version of Old and New Testament accounts is significantly different than in those documents themselves. At every turn, the Qur'an takes an angle favoring the Arabs over the Jews, and it points to the ministry of the eventual Mohammed. The Qur'an's testimony concerning itself, and its statements about the Bible, say that the Old and New Testaments are God's Word, too, but that they have been severely corrupted in copying and translation, and that even in the original manuscripts they were not perfect, due to the immaturity of the people to whom they were given, and their partial understanding of God. How the polytheistic, rude character of sixth century Arabia was any better than the cultural atmosphere of the Hebrews we are not told. According to the teachings of Islam, however, that problem was overcome by direct dictation from heaven.

In his book, *Understanding Islam,* Thomas W. Lippman says:

> The Qur'an purports to be the successor and continuation of the Jewish and Christian Scriptures, incorporating their teachings in a new revelation that gave the people of Arabia an enlightenment previously accorded only to Jews and Christians. But the Bible was written by men, in several languages, and compiled by men over many centuries. Some Christians reject entire books as spurious, and of course Jews reject the entire New Testament, while the Qur'an was written in one language, over a period of twenty years, by one man.[39]

---

[39] Thomas W. Lippman, *Understanding Islam* (New York, Penguin Publishing Group, 1982) 59.

This analysis is meant to be a criticism of the weakness of the Bible, and an emphasis on the superiority of the Qur'an. But the exact reverse is true.

That the Bible has many writers is one of the indications of its inspiration, since the theology of those writers is harmonious and their testimony agrees. That it agrees, though it reflects some two millennia of history and change, is phenomenal. And that it is written in several languages indicates the fact that God is not the God of Jews only, or of the Arabs, for that matter, but of the whole world, and wishes his revelation to be known and understood by all. In particular, the writing of the New Testament in Koine Greek was the deliberate choice of poly-lingual authors who understood that the street language of their day was the best medium to communicate the message of Jesus Christ.

In fact, it is one of the weaknesses of the Qur'an that it latches on to ethnocentricity and implies that outside Arab culture and the Arabic language there cannot be a full appreciation of Islam. We Christians do not know such a God, who would not make his truth equally understood by all people, of whatever race or language.

The cultural connection of Islam to the Arab world continues in the other pillars of their faith, which we will mention briefly.

Prayer

The second pillar is prayer. Muslims are expected to pray five times daily, and usually they prostrate themselves and face Mecca. A holy place to Islam called the Ka'aba (cube) is located in Mecca, the city of Mohammed's birth. It is interesting that this stone was originally a pagan holy place, and was simply "baptized" (as we would say), when Islam conquered Mecca.

Charity

The third pillar is Charity. The social theory of Islam is basically socialistic, and distribution to the poor is a key concept, though not a notable feature of Islamic extremists. Of each person's total possessions, 2.5% is supposed to be given annually to the poor.

Ramadan

The fourth pillar is Ramadan, a month in the Arab lunar calendar during which Muslims fast every day, and eat at night. This fast commemorates the greatest period of Mohammed's wilderness fast and revelation, preceding his entrance to Mecca with the proclamation of Allah as the one God.

Pilgrimage

The fifth pillar is pilgrimage. Each Muslim is to journey to Mecca once in his lifetime, if possible. Once there, he dons garb common to all who approach the shrine, and he prays and worships there.

The Teachings of Islam

The pillars of Islam are really the closest thing to what we might call a plan of salvation for the Muslim. The teachings of Islam about salvation and other matters have the same historical connection to Judaism and Christianity that we have discussed earlier, but Islam differs widely at points. Consider some of the teachings and beliefs of Islam.

Four main areas

The four main areas of teaching in the Qur'an are: Allah, Creation, Man, and the Day of Judgment.

Creation. Islam teaches that the world was created by Allah, as was man; their understanding of this is similar to that of many conservative Christians. Muslims believe that there is coming a day of judgment in which every person will be dealt with according to how well he has lived. The judgment is expected to be preceded or accompanied by several events or signs: the rising of the sun in the west, the appearance of the Beast; the coming of Gog and Magog (all of these have essentially the same meaning as their parallels in Christian theology); the coming of ad Dajjal (a purely Muslim concept); the descent and return of Jesus to Jerusalem; smoke covering the earth; three eclipses; and a fire that breaks out and rounds up all men into one geographical location for the judgment. The one thing sure to destine one for hell is belief in more than one god. According to some versions of Muslim teaching, however, as long as one is monotheistic, even if he is not Islamic, he may go to heaven.

Satan. Muslims believe in a personal Devil and in his angels, whom they believe God created before the earth.

Circumcision. Like Jews, Muslims perform circumcision; but it is interesting to see the different significance invested in their version of it, and to note what it says about their god, Allah. John Alden Williams, in his book, *Islam,* says that circumcision is performed not as a symbol of the removal of sin, as in Judaism, but that "cutting of a part of the body is a part of God's right on us, like the cutting off of the hand of a thief."[40]

Women. Women in Islam are perhaps better off today than in pre-Islamic Arabia, but they are still given half the status of men. They are, according to the Qur'an, to be beaten if rebellious. So-called "honor killings" are probably more frequent than reported. (An honor killing is the murder of a person for shaming his or her Islamic family.) In the more conservative sects women are denied the opportunity of education, must cover their faces in public, and are not even to go out in public without permission from their husbands, or if not accompanied by a man (depending on cultural rules). Men must marry and may have more than one wife but are limited to four; they must treat all their wives equally. In some countries under Islamic rule women are subjected to extreme restrictions on their conduct and freedom of movement.

Force. Muslims in general believe in the use of force to

---

[40] John Alden Williams, *Islam* (New York, George Braziller, Inc., 1961) 122 .

establish a state in which the pursuit of Islam is assured. While the Qur'an in some places deplores force, it recommends it in other passages, and from the beginning of Islam, Muslims used force in spreading their empire, justifying it as a preemptive measure as much as anything.

The Islamic state of Iran and other states in the Middle East today illustrate the vital connection of Islam with force. While it may be argued that the church in the Middle Ages employed force in the Inquisition and the Crusades, those epochs stand out as exceptions to the church's operating method. And, of course, the Crusades were conducted because of the repeated conquering of the Holy Land by Muslims. The force employed by various countries in the Holy Roman Empire may be considered *responsive*.[41] The use of offensive, first-strike force is an ongoing and dominant reality for Islamic nations, however.

Mahdi. Finally, many Muslims believe in the coming of the Mahdi—a reappearance of a great leader of the past, thought by many to be the twelfth Caliph (the civil and religious leader of an Islamic state). In the popular view, the Mahdi is classed by academics with Christ in his second-coming and the Messiah expected by some modern Jews. Novels have been written on this theme, making out one man to fulfill all three expectations.

We come full circle, back to the historical and conceptual conglomerate of Judaism, Christianity, and Islam. But it exists in significant tension:

- The Christian cannot accept Mohammed as a prophet, since Mohammed discounts the authenticity, the highest authority, the unerringness, and the completeness of the Bible alone.
- We cannot accept Mohammed's claims because he denies the deity of Christ, who died and rose again, and who accomplished all that is needed for our salvation on the cross

---

[41] No inference should be drawn here that we excuse the excesses that took place during one or more of the several Crusades conducted.

and in the empty tomb.
- We cannot accept Mohammed or his claims because he presumed to add to, even replace, the Scripture. For various reasons based on the New Testament itself and the overwhelming assertion of the early church, the canon of Scripture is closed.

Mohammed did not intend the Qur'an to be an *addition* to the Bible but a *replacement* of it, which is entirely untenable to the Christian. Islam is in no way a step beyond Judaism and Christianity. Its concepts are deficient in the eyes of both Jews and Christians.

A Step Behind Judaism

To the Arabs of the sixth century, monotheism was novel; but the Jews grew up with the concept of one God. In Abraham's day, if Ishmael had not lived in hostility with his brethren, the Arabs might have been devoted to Jehovah God all along.

Mohammed's startling revelation to Mecca was two thousand years late; and when it came, it took off on a side street with a parallel doctrine that mimics Judaism and Christianity in many ways.

Mohammed's startling revelation to Mecca was two thousand years late; and when it came, it took off on a side street with a parallel doctrine that mimics Judaism and Christianity in many ways:

- The flight of Mohammed and his followers to Medina has been compared to the Exodus of Moses and the Hebrews.
- Charity is 2.5% giving in Islam, and 10% in Judaism—Islam is a step behind.
- The pilgrimage to Mecca roughly parallels the Jewish yearning

to go to Jerusalem (and even in the Christian world there is deep significance attached to going to the Holy Land).

Yet everywhere Islam parallels these things, it falls behind even Judaism in its perception of ideals. And Judaism falls behind Christianity in failing to recognize the fulfilment of its national hopes in the person of *Jeshua Meshiac, Jesou Christou,* Jesus Christ the Son of the Living God.

Doing God One Better

To their eternal peril, followers of Mohammed have, in Islam, sought to do God one better, to do the Bible one better, to do Jesus Christ one better, to surpass what is forever unsurpassable. And because they attempted the forbidden, they have exaggerated a flaw and made it into a faith; but it is a faith that does not save.

One may also conceive of the overall strategy of Islam as the creation of a religion that set out from the first to contradict and deny every major tenet of Judaism and Christianity.

In the 1990s, Americans began to be more acutely aware of Islam, and since 9-11, fundamentalist Islamists have made abundantly clear their hatred of America, Christianity, Judaism, and any system of government that allows freedom of religion. This radicalism has prompted much discussion about whether Islam is a "religion of peace," and much positioning on the part of Muslims as to where they fall on the scale of peace vs. violence. As with all religions, Islam has its nominal followers, its moderately committed, and its fundamentalists.

The fundamentalist Muslim is radical in his devotion to a god he presumes to be identical *in a historical way* with the God of Jews and Christians. But he is mistaken. Allah is not Yahweh; Allah is not the Lord. Allah is a name in a book called the Qur'an, a name on the tongue of a Muslim, a concoction of an Arab mind from the scant knowledge of Bible idioms and the addition of the harsh deities of a desert land. Allah is unique, to be sure: he has claimed millions of followers, and ushered them into eternity without Christ, and without life eternal.

What to Say to a Muslim

It is extremely important for every Christian to be aware of the great need and the lost condition of the followers of Islam. If the opportunity comes the Christian's way, what should he say to his Muslim friend?

Obviously any witness must be tailored to the situation. Muslims are not all the same. Some are not orthodox, while others are strict and well-versed in their faith. In both groups are persons who are either open to discussing either their own faith or Christian faith, and persons who are not the least interested in hearing about Christianity and are even hostile to the very idea of dialogue about Christian beliefs. Numerous books have been written on the subject of Christian witness to Muslims. This book was designed mostly to describe various faiths, and it offers only the suggestion of the Christian's foundational beliefs to keep in mind if conversation with a Muslim friend is possible.

- *Focus on the gospel.* Remember that the simple gospel of Christ has the power to convict of sin and convince of the Savior even without winning other arguments about doctrine. It is possible that a personal testimony about one's own salvation will open the door to faith, bypassing other issues. Keep the focus on Jesus Christ.
- *Bible.* Lay stress on the belief that God's revelation came through the Jews, the Bible, and Jesus Christ. Show what the Bible says about itself, and what claims Jesus made to exclusive Lordship.
- *Christ.* Present the deity of Christ. Christian faith hangs on that issue. A Christian's life should demonstrate the change and the power and holiness that is possible only through a risen, incarnate God, so the Christian's example is very important to

any witness he may attempt.

- *Trinity.* Emphasize the unity of God in three persons. Show the trinity in Genesis 1-2, in the Psalms, at the baptism of Jesus, and in the letters of Paul.
- *Prayer.* Pray for the Holy Spirit to work in the life of a Muslim friend. Only God can turn his life around, make him realize his need of a Savior, and convince him that Savior is Jesus Christ and no other.

Summing up

In the 21st century Islam is a growing force in the United States, and many Muslims are hostile to America in particular and the western world in general. The often unspoken fear of the threat of fundamentalist Muslims makes many Christians reluctant, if not terrified, to broach the subject of their faith in Jesus Christ. As with advice here on witnessing to persons of faiths other than Islam, it is vital to remember that the role any particular Christian plays may be only to sow seed, and that seed may be no more than a single sentence affirming one's faith in Jesus.

Christians and Muslims are, in many ways, miles apart. But remember Paul's words: **I am not ashamed of the gospel, because it is God's power for salvation to everyone who believes (Romans 1:16 HCSB).**

Jehovah's Witnesses
Opponents of the Truth
(2 Timothy 3:5-8)

The average Christian is awed, humbled, and just a little bit afraid, of anyone's dedication to God greater than his own. Anybody who braves rejection and ridicule for handing out tracts in public places, or walks from door to door in a neighborhood on sweltering days for hours, inviting people to talk about the Bible and about God, inspires a kind of respect, curiosity, and suspicion all at the same time. Many people think that the Jehovah's Witnesses are a Christian group that is just more dedicated overall than the average, mainline denomination. Many of us have been told by our elders, "You have to admire their zeal—they are deeply committed."

The Christian, however, need not admire commitment or zeal *per se*. Paul wrote to the Galatians, "Those people are zealous to win you over, but for no good. What they want is to alienate you from us, so that you may have zeal for them" (Galatians 4:17 NIV). Similarly, he wrote to the Roman Christians, "For I can testify about them that they are zealous for God, but their zeal is not based on knowledge" (Romans 10:2 NIV).

In other words, not all zealous commitment is equal; it matters what a person is committed *to*. Commitment to the way of truth arises out of the heart touched by God. Commitment to enemies of the truth arises out of the corrupt heart of sinful man, and is not worthy of either emulation or admiration. Jehovah's Witnesses as a Society and a movement have been one of the most devout enemies of the truth of God this past century has seen, by declaring themselves opponents of key doctrines of genuine Christian faith, and by denouncing all other forms of religion but their own.

God showed the writers of scripture that such enemies of the truth would appear in the last days—and, indeed, they were appearing when the scriptures were written. Paul, writing to Timothy, paints in sweeping literary movements, with dark colors and clashing hues, a picture of these opponents of the gospel and the true revelations of God, partly as a reflection of what he dealt with in his own day, and partly as an assurance to all who would read it that such people would continue to appear, to oppose the true Christ and his people:

> **... [People] having a form of godliness but denying its power. Have nothing to do with them. They are the kind who worm their way into homes and gain control over weak-willed women, who are loaded down with sins and are swayed by all kinds of evil desires, always learning but never able to acknowledge the truth. Just as Jannes and Jambres opposed Moses, so also these men oppose the truth—men of depraved minds who, as far as the faith is concerned, are rejected (2 Timothy 3:5-8).**

Paul predicted the emergence of a type of anti-religion religiosity which is devoid of purifying power: a counterfeit godliness that serves only to perpetuate the lost condition of its followers amid its persuasive error. There could be many particular groups who have emerged since Paul wrote these words that would fit his description well enough to literally fulfill his prophecy. Not many, if any, fit like the Jehovah's Witnesses. This is a call for Evangelicals and *all* true Christians both to beware and to prepare: Beware of the Jehovah's Witness movement, since it is unscriptural and misguided; but prepare yourselves to pray for and work for the conversion of persons entrapped by this spiritually deadly error.

We have implied a strong scriptural basis for the statement that the Witnesses are enemies of God. We should first deal with the previous Bible text to make it more clear why we are so firmly convinced of this. Notice first Paul's term, "a form of godliness." It means an outward presentation—as in the claim to be a religious group. In Paul's day it may have been several groups or prominent figures who put themselves up as something great, but failed the important test: power—the change of heart and life produced by the coming of the living Spirit of God. It is not just *any* change that is desired, but one in which personal sin is dealt with by Christ, and the heart is turned to accept God's truth. Merely becoming dedicated to a cause, starting a movement, even giving your life to it, is just a form, to use Paul's word, and does not guarantee the power. Jehovah's Witnesses are such a movement.

One thing Paul tells us to be on the lookout for is the method of "worming their way into homes." This is not a condemnation of house-to-house witnessing: it is a warning against manipulative techniques, subtle pressure and guilt tactics designed to catch the naive or unsuspecting. The purpose of these tactics, Paul says, is to "gain control." Control does not have to be official. It may be mental, psychological and spiritual. Literally, Paul is talking about someone's "getting a hold on you." This is a perfect description of what Jehovah's Witnesses and other cult groups do.

Finally, Paul gives an especially apt identifying mark: "Always learning but never able to acknowledge the truth." This is a glove-fit adjective for Jehovah's Witnesses and others who fanatically suck up and spit out information received from the approved authority of their group, but who learn little of any value, and will not acknowledge the truth of the genuine word of God, or even read it without the biased spectacles of their cult masters. "These men," says Paul, "oppose the truth." They are sincere, no doubt, and many people excuse them from blame on that account. But they are sincerely wrong, sincerely against God, and sincerely lost, and in desperate need of a real Savior. On that note, let us look at

The Background of the Witnesses

Like so many cults, Jehovah's Witnesses began not as a devout band of the faithful, but with a single man. Charles Taze Russell was born in 1852 in Pittsburgh. He did not react fondly to the strong, harsh Calvinism that surrounded him in his young days, and by his teens he was a skeptic, hardening in human pride. Some Bible doctrines, like that of hell, he disbelieved entirely.

As a young man, and a successful salesman, he decided to study the Bible for himself, so as to work around the unacceptable doctrines of the church. He soon worked out a personal system of interpretation, and organized a Bible study around his method, in 1870. Building on his popularity in this, in 1879 he founded Zion's Watch Tower, a periodical he wrote in its entirety which had a circulation of 6,000 by 1880. Nine years later he founded the Zion Watch Tower Tract Society, to disseminate his materials.

From the start, it was not a church that Russell led, but a movement based on his personal views, which majored in printed material and personal distribution. His main work, which has had a distribution of more than 16 million copies in 35 languages to date, is *Studies in the Scriptures,* a several volume set Russell wrote over a few years time.

His success as a salesman of his personal views was not matched in his personal life. His wife divorced him in 1903 over another woman and Russell's intolerable attitude at home. He was in court several times during his life as a defendant, and on one occasion he perjured himself by lying about knowing how to read Greek—in fact, he had no appreciable knowledge of the original languages of the scriptures. But to those who read his persuasive literature, he was known as "The Pastor." Russell claimed that he was the one who fulfilled Jesus' words in Luke 12:42, which speak of a "faithful and wise servant, whom the master puts in charge of his servants."

When Russell died in 1916, a lawyer by the name of Joseph Rutherford became his successor. He intensified Russell's approach, castigating all religion but the Russellites (as they became known) and attacking all ministers, while characterizing all church history since A.D. 325 as apostate. Rutherford died in 1942, and the Watchtower Bible and Tract Society (Watchtower Society for short), or Jehovah's Witnesses (adopted as their official name in 1931), have been overseen by a series of presidents since.

In 1950 they were officially the fastest growing religious group in America. They operate printing facilities in dozens of localities throughout the world, and they run a short-term Bible school in New York and a radio station. Their real strength is not in their facilities or institutions, but in the vast numbers of common folk putting in hours and hours every week "witnessing"—handing out literature, and going door to door trying to interest people in Bible studies using Watchtower literature. What does that literature teach?

The Doctrines of the Witnesses

Scripture

Jehovah's Witnesses regard the Bible as the word of God. Unlike many cults, Witnesses do not have additional scriptures *per se*, but the writings of Charles Russell serve as the authoritative interpretation of the Bible. Russell wrote in 1910 that if a person had to make a choice between reading the Bible only or reading his *Studies in the Scriptures,* then his book would be preferable. And the Watchtower Society continues, like the papacy of Roman Catholicism, to be the sole source of truth for Jehovah's Witnesses. Under that system of doctrine, the Watchtower Society teaches the following:

God

There is one God, and no trinity. Witnesses hold that Jesus Christ is not *the* God, and that the Holy Spirit is not God, but the impersonal force of God. Jesus is officially believed to have been the angel Michael before his incarnation as Jesus. He is regarded as being the Son of God in the sense of a created being, and in that sense *a god* but not one with *Jehovah* God.

This view of Jesus was what 4th century Arianism asserted, and it was rejected on the basis of firm and accurate exposition of the Bible by the church in A.D. 325, which Witnesses regard as an act of apostasy by the church. This is apparently in direct rejection of comparative teachings of Isaiah 8:13 with 1 Peter 3:15, of Isaiah 6:1-3 with John 12:41, and of Romans 9:5 and 1 John 5:20, to name only a few references.

Jehovah's Witnesses' belief about the Holy Spirit is a contradiction of the teachings of Isaiah 6:9-10 as compared to Acts 28:25 and other passages, and it is based on an ignorance of the fact that the Greek language's word for spirit is neuter, thus forcing the use of neuter *pronouns*[42]—a fact that is outweighed by overwhelming usage of Holy Spirit as a personal designation. Yet, the Watchtower has printed its own Bible, which blatantly ignores the scholarship of translation specialists and renders all passages referring to the Spirit with a small "s."

It is interesting to note that although Witnesses refer to God only by the name Jehovah, the word "Jehovah" is itself a construction dating to about A.D. 1540, by translators of the original Hebrew of the Old Testament. Jews historically would not pronounce the name of God given to Moses on Sinai. That name, in Hebrew, was YHWH (יהוה). The Hebrew alphabet contains no vowels—those were invented by the Masoretic Jews long after the completion even of the New Testament. Since the Jews didn't pronounce the name of God for hundreds of years, the Masoretes had to assign vowels to the Hebrew consonants that belonged to another word, *adonah,* which means "Lord." Jews said "adonah" whenever they came to the name of God. Combining the YHWH of God's name with the vowels of "adonah" gives us "Yahovah, or Jehovah. Yet Jehovah's Witnesses claim that the word "Jehovah" as thus pronounced, is the only authoritative name of God. This is one of the fallacies of not knowing the original languages or using them properly.

---

[42] This is particularly true for word-for-word translations as opposed to dynamic translations.

Man

Jehovah's Witnesses believe man to have been created, not evolved—which is an accurate summation of man's nature; however, their conception of sin is deficient, as they do not believe every man has a deep and abiding problem with sin that can be solved only by a new birth. They hold this in direct contradiction of Jesus' words to Nicodemus,"You must be born again." And Paul taught by the Holy Spirit, "Neither circumcision nor uncircumcision availeth anything, but a *new creature" (Gal. 6:15).*

Atonement

The Witnesses teach that Christ was a ransom for the sins of human beings, meaning that his physical life *only* was required to be given for the original sin of man, but that each person's salvation depends upon the subsequent approach of a man to God, returning to the belief in one, *non-triune* God, and strict adherence to *works* and witness in order to be finally saved.

Heaven and Hell

The Society teaches that there is a heaven, but that only 144,000 people will be there—all of them Jehovah's Witnesses. The rest of the semi-saved will live on a recreated earth, in something less than eternal bliss. Hell, they believe, is not ongoing punishment, but a place of *annihilation*, where those who go pass from existence forever. Death, then, for the Witnesses, results in unconsciousness, until the general resurrections for judgment. (With the exception of Russell, whom Joseph Rutherford stated had gone directly into the presence of God.)

This doctrine is drawn from ignorant readings of Old Testament words for *sheol,* the realm of all the dead, and inconsistent dogmatism about verses in the New Testament, as well as the four principles of Russell himself, who said that an ongoing [eternal] hell is impossible because (1) it is unreasonable; (2) it is repugnant to justice; (3) it is contrary to love; and (4) it is unscriptural.

Just in brief response let us note with respect to these enumerated beliefs that:

(1) The "reasoning" of sinful man itself is corrupted by his rebellious condition, and is no test of the word of God;

(2) Hell is, in fact, demanded by the principle of justice, which insists that every person answer for what he chooses freely to do with his life;

(3) The love of God is not some sappy sentimentalism that gives the rebel what he had *rather* receive for his refusal to repent, but it is instead a deep and sacrificial attitude toward creation that does everything possible to win over the sinner, but which will reluctantly let the stubborn stay outside of love-fellowship forever if that is what they choose; and

(4) There is nothing more scriptural than hell. Jesus taught it; his parables illustrate it; and the apostles believed it. In fact, Jesus said more about hell than he did about heaven. Only a rank and deliberate alteration of the plain meaning of the Bible can account for a different belief using the same texts.

The Resurrection

Witnesses believe that Christ did not rise bodily, but only spiritually, since his human body was a ransom for sin and died forever. Officially, they speculate that the body of Jesus has been preserved for show, perhaps in the millennium. They cite a proof-text from 1 Peter 3:8 about Christ's having been put to death in the body but being raised in the Spirit. But they ignore Luke 24:36-43, where Jesus goes to great lengths to demonstrate that he, in his resurrected state, was human, flesh and bones, who had scars in his hands and side, and who ate like any man.

The Second Coming

Using an ingenious but Biblically unfounded system of

numerology, Witnesses believe that Christ returned to earth in 1914, when the World Wars began, and that he entered his temple—The Jehovah's Witnesses corporately—in 1918, three and a half years later. They believe him now to be reigning in heaven, and planning Armageddon.

In accordance with this view, Witnesses do not call themselves a church; they are simply witnesses, and they meet in Kingdom Halls. Other eschatological views are too complicated to describe fully here, but briefly, they maintain that Armageddon could happen at any moment.

The Society officially predicted Armageddon to occur in 1874; then in 1914, 1925, 1941, 1975, and 1986(ish). Some of their literature now points to 2033 as the year of Armageddon. Re-figuring the date involves changing the system of number shuffling every time, but apparently that does not bother the Watchtower Society. *When* it happens, however, they expect that the millennium will begin, during which almost everybody will eventually turn to Christ—for lack of reason not to. The few who do not will finally be annihilated.

The "other sheep" (John 10:16), whom the Mormons consider to be themselves, the Witnesses regard to be all persons not included in the 144,000 in heaven, who will live eternally here on a recreated earth. There are smatterings of truth in all this; it is a weaving together of truth with fantasy and error—which is what makes it so dangerous for the biblically uninformed.

Ecclesiology

Virtually all Witnesses are ordained ministers, and as such have the privilege of claiming immunity from just about any civic responsibility on the basis of conscientious objection. Such status also includes the responsibility of being quite active in "ministerial" duties, like visitation and distribution of literature. More genuine Christians should do such things; if those who love a lie are successful in promulgating it, how much more should those who love the truth do the same?

And make no mistake, Witnesses are successful. Evangelicals who have high commitment to sending missionaries, such as Baptists, are proud of their missionary success in foreign countries, but Jehovah's Witnesses have more converts than Baptists in Benin, Ghana, Mauritius, Niger Republic, Senegal, South West Africa, Zambia, Japan, Argentina, Barbados, Belize, Chile, Colombia, Costa Rica, Dominica, The Dominican Republic, Ecuador, El Salvador, Grenada, Guadeloupe, Mexico, Peru, Suriname, Trinidad, Uruguay, Venezuela, Austria, Belgium, France, Greece, Italy, Lebanon, Norway, Portugal, Spain, Switzerland, and West Germany, in all of which Baptists and other evangelicals have mission work. In some cases, Witnesses' numbers *vastly* exceed those of Christian denominations.

Evaluation

The truth of God could be known to Jehovah's Witnesses, but it is obscured by the dogmatism, restrictiveness and oppressiveness of their system of "study." Witnesses are discouraged from studying the Bible *on their own*. They must use official Society materials. And the chief ingredient in their materials, perpetuated by the Watchtower Society, which consistently traces back to Charles Russell himself, is a thoroughgoing rationalism—*the subjection of the Bible to the criteria of human reason*.

Russell wrote in *Studies in the Scriptures:*

We have endeavored to uncover the foundation upon which all faith should be built—the word of God—in a manner that will appeal to and can be accepted *by reason as a foundation*. Then we have endeavored to build upon that foundation the teachings of scripture in such a manner that, so far as is possible, *purely human judgment* may try its squares and angles by the most exacting rules of justice which it can command (italics ours).

In bald terms, Jehovah's Witnesses interpret the Bible by

deciding if it matches up with their way of thinking.

But the very concept of revelation is based on the premise that there are things we need to know and believe that we could not conceive without God's giving them to us. To then subject this revelation to our reason, and disbelieve—or *reinterpret*— what we do not like by rationalizing it away, is to destroy the supernatural character of the Bible. That Jehovah's Witnesses speak of the Bible as the word of God must not blind us to this fact: *They do not trust the word of God: they trust themselves and make the Bible reflect their heresies.*

This can be quite confusing, especially when we come up against the apparently contradictory fact that the Witnesses have a number of beliefs in common with conservative Christians. For instance, they consider women to be equal in grace but different in role; they are strenuously against divorce; they oppose abortion; and they firmly reject homosexuality.

One of the strengths of their approach is that they appeal to persons who believe themselves to be basically good, who want to be upstanding and deeply religious, and who are willing to be known as such—even be martyr-like—but who are also *proud* of their desire to be good. And it is this pride that stands in their way: They do not really seek conversion through the power of God. The proud person's approach to the Lord is, "Help me *some,* God, and I will live for you! Reward my goodness and my return to you!" But they don't say, "Have mercy on me, oh God, a sinner!"

The Truth About Jehovah's Witnesses

We must conclude that Jehovah's Witnesses are not Christians in the Biblical sense. Despite their heavy involvement with the Bible and with familiar religious accouterments, and despite their claim that they are persecuted because they are being genuinely Christian, they are spiritually lost. They are those Paul described as "having a form of godliness but denying its power." And that verse says quite plainly, "Have nothing to do with them."

Does that mean ignore them? It cannot—*not* because it is not *reasonable,* but because, *comparing scripture with scripture,* we find Paul also to say that the lost, while not being in close, harmonious fellowship with us, should be the object of our prayer and witness. We are prohibited from thinking of them as brethren and warned against making close ties with them in a manner that might lead to their destructive heresies influencing us. But we must pray for them and seek ways to witness more effectively to them about the *real* Christ and his *real* salvation.

In Guatemala, one of the countries where the Jehovah's Witnesses are stronger than Christian denominations, Southern Baptist missionary Helen Hardeman was in a class on natural childbirth whose instructor was a Jehovah's Witness, named Dona Aida. Helen visited her, and broached the subject of Jesus Christ. Dona launched into a spiel from her training as a Witness.

When Hardeman got in a word, she read some verses straight from the Bible about Christ. Dona gave the official, Watchtower responses, denying the deity of Christ. But finally they agreed to study the matter. Weeks later, Dona left Helen a Watchtower tract attacking the trinity. Helen responded with a visit, and, using even Dona's own Watchtower version of the Bible, the *New World Translation,* showed her where the tract did not match up to the word of God. This time, Dona did not have a pat answer.

When that story was related to Baptists back home, Dona had not yet accepted Christ as Lord and Savior. But Helen said, "She was willing to admit that if Jesus is Jehovah and she refuses to recognize him as such, then she is committing a sin serious enough to affect her eternal destiny." And Mrs. Hardeman added, "Pray for her. It's a frightening thing to admit that your religion has led you away from the truth. It will mean breaking ties with customs, friends and perhaps even family."

Talking with Jehovah's Witnesses

Because of the method Jehovah's Witnesses employ, an Evangelical Christian attempting on any level to witness to a Jehovah's Witness should be prepared for him or her to invoke their own witnessing strategy.

- *Discussion, not disagreement.* Do not become embroiled in argument. If possible, avoid answering "trick" questions, and resist being put on the defensive. If you feel overwhelmed, say that the two of you will have to agree to disagree, and change the subject until another time.
- *Back to the Bible.* Understand that the genuine Christian's source of authority is the Bible, without the interpretations of Charles Russell. Insist courteously that you will rely on what the Bible itself teaches.
- *Preparation.* Be prepared through your own Bible Study. Consult other materials provided by your own denomination to know what Jehovah's Witnesses may say to attempt to trap or confuse Christians. This chapter is not detailed enough for all witnessing encounters. If you are not confident that you can hold your own, defer to someone else who can.
- *Prayer.* Pray for your Jehovah's Witness friend in private. Ask God to use any scripture you may have been able to employ in witness.
- *Patience.* Jehovah's Witnesses who have been part of the movement for a long time may seem thoroughly intractable. Be patient, and seek the help of others, such as ministers, where appropriate.

Summing up

We do not entertain any dreams that several million Jehovah's Witnesses will come flocking into the kingdom through evangelical witness. But maybe a Witness you the reader know will try but fail to change you, but will instead find a change for himself through you, and thereby find life. For it was to *you,* born again through the power of his resurrected life, to whom Jesus said, *You shall be my witnesses.*

Judaism
Way of Law in a Day of Grace
(Romans 9:1-5,30-33,10:1-4)

Looking at Judaism can evoke sadness in a Christian. For Judaism is the faith of God revealed to man and nurtured to the point of fulfilment, but derailed at the apex of its potential.

A woman who worked for a food brokerage company visited one of the stores the company served and picked up some bread dough that was just slightly out of date. She sometimes brought such packages home and made use of them since they weren't spoiled. She put the packages in the back of her station wagon and returned home. Inadvertently, however, she left the dough in her car overnight and throughout part of the next, hot day. When it was discovered, it had burst its bags and was brimming over, looking like some creature out of a cheap horror movie. Of course, at this point the dough was no longer any good. The slightest disturbance made it deflate into a heavy mass, fit only to be discarded.

This is a humorous story, but it illustrates a great tragedy: Judaism was mixed and kneaded by the hand of God, who prepared it to be the source of bread for the whole world's spiritual hunger. But at the appointed hour of its transformation, the bulk of Judaism simply overinflated with the leaven of the Pharisees and became useless to the redeeming plan of God. Only a small number of Jews, a remnant, realized the finishing process and went on to carry the bread from heaven to waiting mankind. The rest of Judaism spiritually collapsed of its own weight and remains so today.

In some limited sociological sense, however, Judaism seems alive and well; but many religions thrive in our world. The continuation of a religion through many years does not in itself recommend it, or prove its authenticity as the way of life before God. Indeed, one of the key things we need to understand about Judaism is that although its formative years coincide with our own spiritual heritage as Christians, it is not, today, what it used to be;

in fact, from the time of Jesus Christ Judaism has ceased to be the avenue of God's revelation and redemptive work in the world. To state its tragic circumstances succinctly, Judaism is a way of law in a day of grace.

It is fitting for us to take a text from Paul's letter to the Roman Christians, where he to explains the point at which nearly all his Jewish brethren missed the boat. There we find the essential facts surrounding their national failure:

> I speak the truth in Christ—I am not lying, my conscience confirms it in the Holy Spirit—I have great sorrow and unceasing anguish in my heart. For I could wish that I myself were cursed and cut off from Christ for the sake of my brothers, those of my own race, the people of Israel. Theirs is the adoption as sons; theirs the divine glory, the covenants, the receiving of the law, the temple worship and the promises. Theirs are the patriarchs, and from them is traced the human ancestry of Christ, who is God over all, forever praised! Amen.
>
> …the Gentiles, who did not pursue righteousness, have obtained it, a righteousness that is by faith; but the people of Israel, who pursued the law as the way of righteousness, have not attained their goal. Why not? Because they pursued it not by faith but as if it were by works. They stumbled over the stumbling stone. As it is written: "See, I lay in Zion a stone that causes people to stumble and a rock that makes them fall, and the one who believes in him will never be put to shame."
>
> Brothers and sisters, my heart's desire and prayer to God for the Israelites is that they may be saved. For I can testify about them that they are zealous for God, but their zeal is not based on knowledge. Since they did not know the righteousness of God and sought to

establish their own, they did not submit to God's righteousness. Christ is the culmination of the law so that there may be righteousness for everyone who believes (Romans 9:1-5, 30-33, 10:1-4 NIV)

Paul passionately proclaimed that the Jews, blessed as they were with every preparation for God's central redeeming work, had rejected it when it appeared. The turning point was the cross; and for that reason Paul preached the cross to his Jewish brethren with all his might, knowing that apart from acceptance of the message of the cross of Christ, there was no hope for the Jews' salvation.

Judaism today, rooted in the Old Testament, reflects the authentic revelation of God up until Christ. But Judaism virtually aborted its divinely appointed mission at that point, missing the original goal as the nation of God's choice.[43] The explicit word from the Lord to Abraham was that "I will bless those who bless you, and whoever curses you I will curse; and *all peoples on earth will be blessed through you*" (Genesis 12:3, italics ours). It is singularly tragic that the ultimate blessing of Jews on the world—to bring into the world the Messiah who gives eternal life—should be rejected by the Jews themselves. We Christians should renew our affirmation of Jesus as the Messiah, Savior of both Jew and Gentile, and revitalize the proclaiming of that faith to Jews in our day.

Preparatory to that renewed evangelism is an examination of the fundamental elements of Judaism and a recognition of the crucial departure of Judaism from the way of truth. To that end we should look at four basic statements. The first is:

---

[43] We do not deal in this book with the sense in which Israel remains the people of God's "historical choice." The eschatological role that Israel may fulfil in the end times is distinct from the "choice" reflected in those people who respond to the gospel, which is rooted in every way in the word of God.

The Basic World View of Judaism is Shared with Christians

God

The thing that most distinguished ancient Judaism from other religions of its time was its monotheism. While other cultures and nations had a god for the sun and a god for the moon, one for the rain and one for the sea, one for every phenomenon almost, the Jew realized that life was devoid of harmony and divested of meaning in polytheism. In her history, Israel had come face to face with one, living, sovereign God; and her commitment to that God, Yahweh, was official, if marred by frequent unfaithfulness.

References to "gods" in places such as Psalm 82 and Deuteronomy 32, and to "sons of God" in passages such as Job 1:6 and 2:1 (in Hebrew) speak of *created heavenly beings* that were part of God's heavenly council or had a role in administering government of the earth. But the people of Israel early realized that their God, Yahweh, was the only infinite being, the only deity, and the only one who must be worshiped and obeyed.

Even considering the times in the wilderness experience or during the time of the judges when the worship of Baal or of other gods was going on, it is the record of Jewish history that such incidents are regarded as serious diversion from the truth: "Hear, O Israel: The Lord our God, the Lord is one. Love the Lord your God with all your heart and with all your soul and with all your strength" (Deuteronomy 6:4-5 NIV). The word "one" in verse 4 means "unique."

Creation

Just as evident as the fact of one and only one God was the conviction, brought about through revelation, that God was responsible for this universe and all life. "In the beginning, God created the heavens and the earth" (Genesis 1:1). Not only did he create it, but it is therefore good: "And God saw all that he had made, and behold, it was very good" (Genesis 1:31). To this day, one of the marks of Judaism is its appreciation of creation. In the best sense of the word, Judaism is an "earthy" religion. Christians share with Jews the basic truth that even salvation includes the prospect of the redemption of the whole creation: God is not going to surrender the created order to Satan, while salvaging the spiritual dimension of it alone. This was the prophetic urgency of Job when he declared, "In my *flesh* I shall see God."

Man

Concerning man himself, Judaism regards him as the crown of creation, characterized by a bonding of spirit and flesh into an unified being: God "breathed into his nostrils the breath of life, and man became a living soul" (Genesis 2:7). "You made him a little lower than the heavenly beings and crowned him with glory and honor" (Psalm 8:5). That last bold assertion is not bold enough in its translation, since the Hebrew says, "You made him a little lower than God." Jews and Christians agree: Man is God's noblest creation.

Yet, man is a sinner. Though Jewish theology today is not identical with Christian beliefs on this point, there is a shared idea of man as "missing the mark," as he lives out his life. As Huston Smith put it in his book, *The Religions of Man,* "Meant to be noble, they are usually something less; meant to be generous, they withhold from others. Created more than animal, they often sink to being nothing else."[44]

History-Revelation

Finally, Jews and Christians today share the common realization that in the Hebrew people of old and through Israel the nation, God was active in revealing himself to the world. The scriptures Christians know as the Old Testament are the record of

---

[44] *The World's Religions,* 281.

a history that breathes with the evident working of God. The Jew believes, as the Christian does, that in ancient history God was shaping the order of events in such a way as to instruct anyone who was willing to be taught by that revelation. God himself is revealed as a being of infinite power, boundless love, and intimate involvement with his creation.

In all these ways, the cosmology common to most Jews today is either identical or very similar to that of Christians. After all, our spiritual roots are the same.

Traveling to Israel for a tour of "The Holy Land" can be dangerous at times. Nevertheless, many Christians have done so over the years. One minister who took such a tour with a group of other ministers and church members wrote the following upon his return:

> It was the most unusual, exciting and memorable trip I have ever experienced. Reflecting on that experience, I have noted many times since how much at home I felt there, in Jerusalem, by the shores of the Galilee, among this people whose language I did not understand (even after studying it!). I was left with the distinct impression that the only reason I felt that way was that I sensed the underlying commonality of our heritage in the God of revelation. The land was filled with the images and impressions of a scripture I hold dear as do the Jews; and going there was like going home to a place where I had never been.

The commonality of Christians with Jews does not end with the rudimentary concepts on which Judaism is based. Since the whole of our Old Testament is shared with the Jews, it is well for us to give some thought to a second characteristic of Judaism:

The Teachings of Judaism Underlie Christian Thought

Within the framework of the basic world view of Judaism, there are several teachings that characterize both the ancient and the modern faith. One of these is the concept of:

Morality. By rabbinical count, there are 613 commandments in the Jewish scriptures, our Old Testament, regulating behavior. Most of these are located in the first few books of the Torah; and chief among them all are the Ten Commandments, given by God through Moses. The commandments relating to interpersonal behavior cover four things that are apt to be the most trouble to human beings: money and possessions, sex, the use of force, and the tongue. The Ten Commandments draw the line in these areas and define the inevitable result of wrong attitudes relating to each. Greed leads to covetousness which leads to stealing; lust leads to promiscuity which leads to adultery; anger leads to fighting which leads to murder; and guilt leads to defensiveness which leads to deceit.

The moral principles in the Ten Commandments underlay the teaching of Jesus himself, who instructed his hearers: "You have heard it said that you should not commit adultery,' but I am telling you that if you lust you have already committed 'heart-adultery,'" and so on. These truths were powerfully taught in Jesus' ministry as no one had taught them before, but they are found in the overall fabric of the Old Testament in their entirety.

Justice. Another major teaching of Judaism that underlies Christian doctrine is justice. It was the typical subject of the ministries of the prophets. Of the early, "guild" sort of prophet we do not have many records of their utterances. But by the time of the individual prophets such as Nathan, Elijah and Elisha, the non-writing prophets, we have encounters with kings and commoners reflecting the call of God for justice in the affairs of men. Nathan stands in the presence of David and calls the king to account for the virtual murder of Uriah, whose wife Bathsheba David wanted for himself. The prophet was revered, respected, sometimes feared in Israel, and the nation knew that God spoke through him.

Judaism today does not have any contemporary prophets. Nor does it claim any since the days of the Old Testament; for that matter, neither does Christianity, in the specific sense of the Old Testament type. But the Old Testament prophets, still authoritative to the Jew of today, are the precursors of the New Testament apostles and preachers. The New Testament gift of prophecy was that enablement given to the proclaimer of the word of God; every God-called preacher today operates in the spirit of the prophets in that limited sense, and his ministry reflects the age-old ways of God in sending a crying-voice into the midst of humanity.

Election and Suffering. The ideas of election and suffering are also parents to New Testament theology. Jews have always regarded their nation to have been chosen of God for a special purpose, and the suffering they underwent as a slave nation, a vassal nation and then a dispersed nation, are regarded in an almost redemptive light. God chose Israel to be his channel of revelation, and that process of revelation involved suffering. As Huston puts it, "It was a *teaching* experience for them and a *redemptive* experience for the world."[45] This is the typical, modern Jewish interpretation of the great 53rd chapter of Isaiah, which speaks of the suffering servant. But it translates directly into a description of Jesus Christ, as revealed in the historical narratives of the New Testament. Again, the stage for the work of God which would usher in faith in Christ, was set in the centuries of Israelite experience and revelation.

But at this point, we must begin to see the divergence of Judaism from the truth. Whereas our first two statements were affirmations of Jewish faith, our last two distinguish the way of

---

[45] *The World's Religions,* 294.

truth in Christ Jesus from the parent faith:

The Unbelief of Judaism
Is Its Crucial Error

Undeniably, one of the strongest convictions of Jews between 100 B.C. and A.D. 30 concerned the coming of a deliverer. To some, this was a matter of prayer, and to others, a matter of revolution. The messianic expectancy grew up out of the words of the prophets back as far as Moses and from a corresponding sense of need brought about by forces of oppression, like the Roman Empire. The problem was that the Jewish expectations were so deeply colored by their social and political predicament that when the Messiah appeared, they did not recognize him.

Jesus was called the Christ (Greek for 'Messiah') by both his followers and himself (Mt.26:63-64) and he demonstrated in his flawless and miraculous life that he was anointed of God uniquely. A small band of Jewish men and women believed he was the Messiah for whom they had waited. But "the Jews" (meaning most of them, and particularly the leadership) violently rejected this claim and asserted the opposite—that he was an agent of Satan. Consequently they had him crucified. But Jesus did not stay in the tomb. He was resurrected by the power of the Spirit of God. This is the unanimous and forceful message of the New Testament writings, the report over 500 persons who saw him risen and in his body, and the proclamation of the whole New Testament church. It has been pointedly observed that Jesus' followers could not have received from a *dead Savior* the transformation obviously worked on them, a transformation that has powerfully motivated the church ever since.

Instead of believing in Jesus as Messiah, the Jews looked for another. But one was not to be found. The plight of Judea became worse and worse up to the end, which was the complete subjection under Titus, the destruction of the Temple, and the eventual dispersion of the nation. The Jews had failed to listen to their newly come prophets, the apostles, who proclaimed, "When God raised up his servant, he sent him first to you to bless you by turning each of you from your wicked ways" (Acts 3:26 NIV).

God offered all Israel a sin sacrifice in Jesus Christ, and he was rejected. In our description of Judaism so far we have not yet mentioned sacrifice, and there was a good reason. The ancient Jews participated in a sacrificial system that dominated their life for most of the Old Testament period—why did we not mention it when speaking about the foundational truths or teachings of Judaism? We did not simply because it is not a part of *modern* Judaism. It has not been a part of Judaism since A.D. 70 when the temple in Jerusalem was destroyed. It is significant that the disappearance of the sacrificial system in Judaism coincides with the emergence of the Christian church. Barely a generation stands between the crucifixion of Christ Jesus and the elimination of Jewish sacrifice.

For the Christian, the meaning is evident: Christ was and is eternally the sufficient sacrifice for all sin; all superficial and symbolic sacrifice ceased when the Jews rejected the perfect Lamb of God.

Meanwhile, the Jews developed other authorities for their continued worship, which are in place today as near-scriptural in authority for conservative and orthodox Jews. The Talmud, a compendium of commentary on the Torah, extra-canonical law and history and tradition, is one of these sources, and the Midrashim (a similar collection) is another.

These sources, along with the all-important Torah (Genesis through Deuteronomy) began to be taught in synagogues—the localized replacements of the Jerusalem temple—and continue to be memorized and mulled over today. Even before the final temple-destruction, prayer, ritual, and the study of the Law had begun to replace an active sacrificial practice. The Levitical priesthood gave way to the Rabbis, and in this way a sadly apparent truth became institutionalized: the living relationship of

Jews to God through a means of mediation had evaporated and left only the powerless repetition of ancient law, with no life in it.

Consequently, as the living revelation was left behind and the final and complete sacrifice foretold in the symbol of the Passover was spurned, Judaism lapsed into the perpetuation of ineffectuality. What before Christ was a powerful, positive faith in a world of impotent fallacies now quickly became a hopeless holdout of never-to-be-fulfilled dreams. Such a religion becomes unavoidably negative. Of the 613 precepts counted so legalistically by the Rabbis, 365 are negative, while only 248 are positive.

Though these precepts are a part of *our own scriptures,* God has shown us that we are not to live in bondage to them, for Christ has fulfilled them all and brought to pass a new way of life through the inward filling and guidance of his Spirit. In Christ, everything becomes *yes!* We do not live by the *no* of murder, but by the *yes* of forgiveness. We are not bound to the *no* of theft, covetousness or adultery, but are free in the bonds of love. The chains of Israel in Babylon or under Rome were nothing compared to the bondage of Israel under the law.

Judaism continues to observe Rosh Hashanah, the new year, with its Day of Atonement; but the Christian lives in the Kingdom with atonement as a reality.

Judaism observes the Feast of Tabernacles, but the Christian celebrates the real, inward dwelling of the Spirit of God in him.

Judaism solemnizes Passover, remembering the Exodus from Egypt; but the Christian feeds on the Living Bread, who once-for-all redeemed him from sin.

Judaism observes Pentecost, Hanukkah and Purim; but Christianity has the present spiritual harvest, the Light of humanity and the power of deliverance which those feasts represent.

In all these observances, the crucial error of Judaism is its unbelief: They seek righteousness by the works of the Law and not by faith. The Jewish concept of sin does not admit its condition as a disease which must be cured by the Christ; the Jew does not believe he needs conversion or redemption, but only improvement—and for that he turns to the Law. But the Spirit speaks through the apostles to say, "No one will be declared righteous in God's sight by the works of the law" (Romans 3:20 NIV). "For by grace are ye saved through faith" (Ephesians 2:8). "Not by works, so that no one can boast" (Romans 2:10 NIV).

This is the heart of the fourth and final statement we must make concerning Judaism; and it is a plea to every Christian heart to grow in concern for the Jewish people in our world:

The Salvation of Jews is Still Only in Jesus Christ

A common misconception based on Romans 9-11, especially 11:26, is that Jews will somehow not have to accept Christ, or that they will have some opportunity after the second coming to accept him almost while in transit to the eternal realms. Paul said nothing of the kind. He simply foresaw a time in the future when there would be a great turning of Jews to Christ, under the powerful preaching of Christian witnesses—probably Jewish Christians themselves.

Paul also foresaw an eventual fulfilment of prophecies concerning national Israel, unchanged by the present age of the largely Gentile church and Judaism in spiritual shambles. But he shows that God conditions this national return to God's favor on *belief!* Paul says:

> "If they do not persist in unbelief, they will be grafted in, for God is able to graft them in again. After all, if you were cut out of an olive tree that is wild by nature, and contrary to nature you were grafted into a cultivated olive tree, how much more readily will these, the natural branches, be grafted into their own olive tree?" (Romans 11:23-24 NIV).

We are the circumcision, who worship God in the Spirit and

who have no confidence in the flesh. We are stewards of the truth of the gospel, the good news of Christ who is the end of the law to all them that will believe. Our abiding command is to tell that good news to everybody. For all are lost without Christ! The Jew is not immune to the judgment of God; he is not excepted from the requirement of personal trust in Christ. Jesus said to his fellow countrymen, the people of his own heritage, his brethren in the flesh, "…unless your righteousness surpasses that of the Pharisees and the teachers of the law"—a righteousness they hoped to acquire through rigid compliance with Old Testament law— "you will certainly not enter the kingdom of heaven" (Mt. 5:20 NIV).

Witnessing to Jews

Presenting the gospel to a Jew may be more difficult for most Christians than presenting it to any other group described in this book. For what separates Jew from Christian is the firm refusal to recognize Jesus of Nazareth as the Jewish Messiah. If you plan to try witnessing to a Jewish acquaintance or friend:

- *What kind of Jews?* Recognize that Jews are not all the same. Some Jews are orthodox—they are faithful worshipers, know their scriptures in varying degrees of excellence, and may be able to argue their position by using the Old Testament. But some Jews are nominal in their faith, though they still hold to the basics of Jewish belief. And finally, while it may seem amazing, some Jews are only so in nationalistic or racial respects, and may actually be atheistic. Try to identify where your Jewish friend falls on the spectrum.
- *Bible preparation.* Be prepared to use Old Testament scriptures in your conversation. Brush up on your knowledge of messianic passages in the Psalms and the prophets, especially Isaiah. Realize that many Jews have never read Isaiah 53, the most messianic passage in the Old Testament, because it has been left out of their lectionary (what is read in synagogue services) for many years.

- *Don't offend.* Try not to refer to the Jewish scriptures as "the Old Testament," unless they do. Call it "the Scriptures," or even "the Tanakh," if you are comfortable with that. Avoid other terms that might offend if another would be just as good.
- *Bible preparation.* Study up on the discussion of Paul in Romans 9-11. Study Hebrews. Look for ways to inject the arguments of the Bible itself into your conversation.
- *Spiritual power.* Rely on the Holy Spirit to use his inspired word to transmit truth to your Jewish friend.

Summing up

Understand Judaism; love the Jews; pray for their conversion; tell the gospel to a Jewish friend! What joy it will be to see Jews completed in Jesus! What glory for a Jewish friend to find the one his people once rejected. And how much more fitting it is for a Jew than even a Gentile: "For theirs are the patriarchs, and from them is traced the human ancestry of Christ, who is God over all, forever praised, Amen!" (Romans 9:5 NIV).

Mormonism
Another Gospel
(2 Timothy 3:14-17)

Many people's first introduction to Mormons has been by exposure to the music of The Mormon Tabernacle Choir. This huge choir has long been a popular among Christians of many stripes. Since the invention of LP vinyl records, The Mormon Tabernacle Choir has been known for its superior versions of hymns, anthems, and seasonal music—such as Christmas. We all learn eventually that the choir is that of the Church of Jesus Christ of Latter Day Saints. We know them by the shorter name: Mormons. But many of us know little more about this religious group than that they sing memorable Christmas music. In fact, a lot of people think Mormons are just another denomination of Christianity. But who are they, really? What are their beliefs? And finally, how should Christians relate to Mormons?

Its History

The Mormon movement began in 1830 with the publication of the *Book of Mormon.* The document was submitted for publication by Joseph Smith, who claimed that it was a translation of golden plates, which he also claimed he found at the direction of an angel named Moroni.

Smith was the son of Joseph and Lucy Mack Smith, both of whom practiced magic and dealt in the occult. Young Joseph was known to have dabbled in divination and fortune telling himself, using magic "peep stones" as his oracles. He said that when he was fifteen he had a vision in which he was told to avoid all churches, since they were in error. Three years later, he said he had a vision in which an angel named Moroni gave him directions to find some golden plates, and a pair of magic spectacles, the Urim and Thummim, by which he would be able to translate them.

By 1827 Smith had married and convinced his new wife and

some others to finance his search for the plates. Then he reported he had unearthed them in the hills near Palmyra, New York, while all alone. Also alone, he went about translating them. No one else ever saw any plates or can testify as to the verity of Joseph Smith's accounts.

The "Book of Mormon," the resulting work, purports to be the history of a branch of Hebrew people who sailed to South America in 600 B.C., settled and migrated and spread into North America. Two camps developed, the Lamanites and the Nephites, and the latter, the faithful, were wiped out by the former. The Lamanites were then cursed with darker skin, which explains the origin of the American Indian, according to the accounts. The last of the Nephites, Mormon and his son Moroni,[46] gathered the records of the faithful and wrote them on golden plates. That was supposed to have been around A.D. 384. Fifteen hundred years later, Joseph Smith claims Moroni appeared to him to tell him of the plates.

Using this Book of Mormon as his basis of belief, Smith organized "the Church of Christ," in April of 1830, with six members. Before a month was out, there were forty. A year later, there were a thousand. They sent out four missionaries, who went to Ohio, and persuaded a former Campbellite (Disciples of Christ) preacher named Rigdon of their beliefs. He led his 127-member congregation to join, too.

With a new base of support farther west, Smith, who was experiencing trouble in Fayette, New York, led sixty followers out to Ohio. This was where Brigham Young joined the movement, and also where Smith secured some Egyptian papyri from which he said he translated what is called "the Book of Abraham."

They went on to settle for a while in Missouri, and then in Illinois in 1839. By this time, they were about 1,000 in number. Within five years, serious dissent had arisen against Smith, and the

---

[46] Mormons believe Moroni was the last of the ancient prophets, who was resurrected and who became an angel.

newspaper of the Mormon community itself was sharply critical of him. Smith had the last edition collected and burned, and the newspaper office destroyed. But there was apparently substance to some of the charges, including those of polygamy and even treason, and Smith and his brother were arrested. They were killed by a mob that stormed the jail.

In the wake of Smith's death, Brigham Young was elected the leader, and he promptly led in a mass exit of 2,000 members from this hotbed of hostility to Utah in 1846. There they carved out their own territory, and in the thirty years before Young's death, they grew to be over 140,000 in number.

During Brigham Young's tenure polygamy was authorized and promoted, and the Tabernacle in Salt Lake City was built. Today, there are five million or so Mormons spread among 75 countries of the world.

This is something of the background against which we are obliged to understand Mormonism. But what makes Mormons distinctive? Is it merely the belief in a migration of Jews and the consequent origin of American Indians? The Book of Mormon says far more. Just what *do* Mormons believe?

Before summarizing Mormon beliefs, consider a Bible passage that speaks of the inspiration of the scriptures:

> **But as for you, continue in what you have learned and have become convinced of, because you know those from whom you learned it, and how from infancy you have known the Holy Scriptures, which are able to make you wise for salvation through faith in Christ Jesus. All Scripture is God-breathed and is useful for teaching, rebuking, correcting and training in righteousness, so that the servant of God may be thoroughly equipped for every good work.(2 Timothy 3:14-17 NIV).**

As we list some primary Mormon teachings, be alert for

contradictions to truths already revealed in the Bible.

Its Doctrines

Authority for its Teachings

The crucial difference between Christian doctrine and Mormon doctrine is that Mormons hold The Book of Mormon superior to the Bible. They say that the Bible is the word of God insofar as it is translated correctly, but they believe it is riddled with errors in translation and transcription. The Book of Mormon they hold to be the reformed guide, perfect in every way. They also accept documents like *The Pearl of Great Price,* and *Doctrines and Covenants,* which are self-ascribed revelations to Smith. Among the things contained in these works, which Mormons believe, are these:

There are several gods. To be frank, Mormons are polytheistic, not monotheistic. Their views of the trinity reveal this fact. While many critics of Christian doctrines call our concept of the trinity polytheism, it is not.[47] However, the Mormon concept of the "trinity" actually *is* polytheistic. They believe the Father, Son and Spirit are three gods, not one God in three persons. This is technically known as Tritheism. The divine triumvirate was said to have elected the Father to be main God, and chosen Christ to come to earth. The Father, called simply, God, is believed to have physical form. He has this because, as they believe, he was once a man, and attained godhood by being exalted.

Jesus Christ was half God, half man. This is the best way to describe the result of Jesus' entrance into the created world. To the Mormon, Jesus Christ was the result of actual physical mating between the Father God and Mary. (This heresy was dealt with by

---

[47] "Trinity" actually is a combination of "tri-" and "unity," meaning a unity of the three.

the church early in first century.) Before Christ's earthly birth he was in heaven, the son of the Father and a heavenly wife. After Christ's experience at Calvary and his resurrection, but before his ascension, he is said to have appeared to the faithful Nephites here in North America (answering common questions about what he may have done in the forty days he was still on earth after the resurrection). During his North American visit he declared the gospel—the Mormon version of it, of course.

Man was pre-existent and may become a God. Man is supposed to try to rise to the perfection of Christ, and so obtain a higher level in the age to come.

Salvation is virtually universal, though multi-leveled. The Mormon believes that even the unrepentant will be saved in a basic way, with only those having committed the unpardonable sin being left out of some conceivable salvation. But the full blessing only comes to those who are in the church, are married in Mormon temples, and live exemplary lives. Baptist listeners would be in a second level of heaven, the Terrestrial one, reserved for members of other religions who did not become Mormons.

Other miscellaneous beliefs. Mormons believe one may be baptized for his pre-1830 dead ancestors, resulting in their salvation. They also hold that Christ will return at or near Independence, Missouri. They believe that doing good works and not doing bad ones is the chief ingredient in salvation. And they hold that Christ died on the cross for Adam's sin, but you have to answer for your own.

How do we evaluate these beliefs? We evaluate them in the light of Scripture, of course, and it is precisely that point where we first come into conflict with the Mormons. They accept different scripture. They do not simply have different interpretations—they have different sources.

Note this above all: When a Mormon says, God, Jesus, Holy Spirit, salvation, scripture, baptism, etc., he has an entirely different thing in mind from the orthodox Christian's beliefs. And several of these words and doctrines must be strictly construed for a person to be a genuine Christian in the first place. Let's review the Mormon's source of authority.

Its source of authority

The Mormon's source of authority is the Book of Mormon, which we have already noted had its origins in the private, unwitnessed work of Joseph Smith. No one else had the information he claimed to be privy to; no one else witnessed the finding or translation of the golden plates. There is no multiple witness, therefore, and we have only the word of a man who was known to dabble in the occult, for this most significant "revelation."

Moreover, the manuscripts that were purported to be the lost Book of Abraham were themselves lost but discovered in 1968, and translated. The translation was done by one of the Mormon's own, and corroborated by other Egyptologists, and reveals that the documents were nothing more than Egyptian burial documents and rituals, and bore no similarity to the English work by Smith. That translator's name was Nelson, and he shortly left the Mormon church.

The Book of Mormon itself is sinking fast under the burden of proof against the emerging facts that it is a gross plagiarism of other works, including both the Bible and also a novel by Solomon Spaulding, who died in 1816. The Spaulding connection was brought up during Smith's own lifetime by contemporaries who noted similarities in content and details between the Book of Mormon and Spaulding's novel, "Manuscript Found." The theory was, of course, refuted by the Mormon Church, and supposedly laid to rest, but a recent flurry of intensive investigation has produced solid evidence from handwriting experts that manuscripts by Spaulding and manuscripts by Smith are done by the same person.

This is all in addition to the patent fact that the whole of the book of Mormon is written in a style similar to the King James Version of the Bible, and it contains many passages that are *direct quotes* of the Bible. For instance, portions of the Book of Mosiah are right out of Isaiah 53, and 3 Nephi 13:1-8 is identical to Matthew 6:1-23.

This identical correspondence might not unsettle Mormons since they believe that the Book of Mormon is the restored, perfect word of God. They say the Bible is thoroughly flawed in its preservation and translation. But if that were so, why would the Book of Mormon contain numerous passages from it? Not only are they from the Bible, but they are from the King James Version, which was not translated until A.D. 1611, while the original version of the Book of Mormon was supposed to have been completed in A.D. 384.

It is interesting to note also that this "most perfect of books" has had more than 2,000 textual changes performed on it since its publication in English in 1830.

All these things probably have fixed and practiced answers by Mormons who are not to be convinced of anything else—and you have to assume that they, like anyone, will defend their beliefs. To be fair, many people level accusations against the Bible, too, and Christians defend their beliefs.

But it does not take much time to display enough evidence to convince us that the Book of Mormon is the work of one man, not an ancient collection of history; that it is a self-contradictory amalgamation of other persons' ideas, not a revelation from God.

It fails three basic tests of divine revelation: an inherent, spirit-inspired self consistency; a consistency with previous sacred revelations in Christian history, and the evoking of devotion and discipleship to the person of Christ.[48]

It becomes unnecessary to evaluate the other doctrines of the Church of Jesus Christ of Latter Day Saints—the Mormons, after dealing with their source of authority. Since their beliefs are derived principally from the Book of Mormon, debating the interpretation of Biblical texts is virtually without purpose. Mormons use the Bible, in the words of one of their own educators, to prove the truth of the Book of Mormon. It is what Paul calls forcefully, "another gospel," as he warns in Galatians, "But even if we *or an angel from heaven* should preach a gospel other than the one we preached to you, let them be under God's curse" (Galatians 1:8 NIV).

- The Bible says God is one, and it reveals this one God in three persons: Father, Son and Spirit.
- The Bible says man was created by God as a new being, that he did not pre-exist.
- The Bible says man sinned, and came under condemnation, which, if he does not receive personal deliverance and salvation from it, will result in his death *in* sin, and unto eternity outside of God—hell.
- The Bible says Christ is the eternal Word of God made flesh, born of a virgin, not a concubine of God.
- According to the Bible, Jesus the man was newly created in Mary's womb, born as any of us, lived perfectly, died on a cross for the sin of every one of us, and was raised from the grave bodily.
- The Bible implies Jesus spent forty days in the region where his ministry was performed, then ascended into heaven and commanded that the gospel be preached to all people including Jews and Samaritans, and all other persons in the world.
- That gospel says that all have sinned and come short of the

---

[48] *Saints and the Baptist Witness*, (Nashville, Home Mission Board, SBC, 1975) 6.

glory of God, that the wages of sin is death eternal, but that the gift of God is forgiveness and life to all who will call on Jesus' name, believing that he died for them and rose from the grave, and naming him Lord of their lives.

- The Bible says that this salvation is not of works, lest any person should boast, but by the grace of God in the finished work of Christ, and is received through faith in Christ—which means trusting his work on our behalf and turning our lives over to him in confidence that he responds with forgiveness and the gift of the Holy Spirit.
- The Bible says Christ is coming again, but it says he will be seen the world around, and will make his presence known uniquely in Jerusalem, and that this event could come about at any time.

What the Bible says has not changed and will not change, and is true, in opposition to all the fabrications of other religions, including the Book of Mormon.

What do you say, then, to persons who have been caught up in the Mormon religion?

Witness To Mormons

You can certainly use some of the reasoning we have offered above. But whatever you do, or have opportunity to do, here are some things to remember:

- *Firm stance.* Mormons need to know that you are a Christian, that you believe the Bible, that you are convinced that it, and it alone, is the word of God, and that you take your beliefs only from it.

  Almost without doubt, attempting to argue about many issues that are ultimately based on religious convictions is mostly if not absolutely fruitless when you and your Mormon acquaintance have different sources of authority. A person who does not believe the Bible to be the only authoritative written word of God usually cannot be won over quickly to an orthodox Christian belief, because his or her source of authority—whether science or philosophy or another religious book or whatever—says otherwise.

If you are not thoroughly read on the Book of Mormon or trained in defending the Bible's being the authority for faith and practice, it is better for you to refer your Mormon friend to written sources on the subject. Perhaps you can purchase such a book and make a gift of it. When you go home, pray that the book will be effective!

- *Loving attitude.* Your Mormon friend or acquaintance needs to know that God loves them, and wants to bring them to salvation, which is through Jesus Christ alone.

Love is attractive and winsome, and some people are far less moved by energetic intellectual conversation than they are by loving friendship and self-evident concern for them.

- *Preparation.* You need to know what you are talking about before conversing with a Mormon, especially a missionary.

Teams of Mormon missionaries who go house to house in the city are indoctrinated and trained, and will not be easily led off course in their mission, which is to get you interested in the Church of Jesus Christ of Latter Day Saints. If you *do* attempt to engage a Mormon in your presentation of the gospel, you need to take, and keep, the offensive, rather than the defensive. Remember that you are in the conversation about faiths so that you can tell him of the Bible way of salvation, not be led into doubt about your own. If it seems useful to you, you could have short pamphlets at hand with the plan of salvation. They might express your beliefs better than you think you could on short notice.

- *Bible knowledge.* Remember that Mormons learn to interpret the Bible in a vastly different manner than Christians in general do.

They have identified proof-texts in the Bible to help authenticate the Book of Mormon. Such verses as John 10:16

are called on as supposed references to God's people on the American continents. While this verse is made to sound obscure, it refers to the Gentiles, as opposed to the Jews, who would believe and be saved. Other texts are reinterpreted different from their authentic meaning, in the light of Joseph Smith's teachings and in the Book of Mormon and the other documents. It is of no value to argue these points. Doctrines like baptism for the dead, or levels of salvation and heaven, need not be debated, because they are not in the Bible; they come from a source the biblical Christian cannot accept.

• *Sober reminder.* Remember that Paul wrote, "Do not go beyond what is written" (1 Cor. 4:6), and Christ told John to warn us, "If anyone adds anything to the words of this book God will add to him the plagues described in this book" (Rev. 22:18). That applies equally to the whole of the Bible, and it takes some mental contortion to justify the addition of, or replacement by, another set of writings, like the Book of Mormon.

Summing up

Many of you have Mormon friends. They *can* be won to Christ—it takes prayer, power, reliance on the miracle working of the Holy Spirit, along with some solid preparedness on your part. Be aware that you *may or may not* be the instrument God will use to lead a Mormon to Christ. Some prepare the ground, some sow seed, some water, and some reap. To be ready for your role, if any, you should know your Bible and what it means, so that you will be equipped to witness to anyone who does not know Jesus as you know him.

Mysticism
Foreign Gods
(Acts 17:16-23)

One of the more confusing things to people in the United States was the introduction of Oriental religions into what were traditionally European cultures. Eastern mysticism—a term we will use inclusively of various, non-Christian spiritual concepts mostly from the eastern hemisphere—has made deep inroads into the United States and other western countries, particularly since the middle of the 20th century. Our responses have been divided. Some see the trend as a broadening of our world view; some see it as the invasion of foreign soil.

Many people who accept the idea of evolutionary anthropology assume that the major races and cultures of man arose more or less independently of each other, and that therefore no one should pass judgment on another culture or the religion of that culture. Christians cannot take such a view and still be evangelical, because the cornerstone premises of Christian doctrine are that there is one God, one true faith, that all have sinned, and that all are lost without salvation from God through Jesus Christ. These core doctrines of Christianity are not shared by eastern, mystical religions.

The Bible teaches that all men are from common stock—God made the first couple and placed them in the Garden of Eden, which was somewhere in the vicinity of what we know as the Fertile Crescent, in the Middle East. From there, the population of man grew. It had not spread far when God sent a great flood to judge the horrific and rampant sin of man. One family, and only one, was spared in this global catastrophe—Noah's. From Noah's sons and their families the whole earth was populated. This includes the lands of India and China, whose cultures are ancient, but stem from roots common to them and to Israel, and, ultimately, the whole world.

The common ancestry of man means that since God inaugurated his truth in Eden, all differing ancient religions today are ancient departures from the truth God revealed. On that basis we can look at religions of the world and evaluate them in the light of the written word of God.

Far eastern cultures were cut off early from communication with the Middle East, however, and throughout the time of the writing of the Bible, there was virtually no knowledge of some of those cultures, particularly China. The Bible does not make direct statements on the particulars of far eastern religions; but some of Paul's words apply well to all variations from the truth. In Acts we have an account of Paul's famous introduction to the men of Athens. Here in this center of pagan thought and endless philosophy, Paul presented the gospel. See how he opened the door of communication.

While Paul was waiting for them in Athens, he was greatly distressed to see that the city was full of idols. So he reasoned in the synagogue with both Jews and God-fearing Greeks, as well as in the marketplace day by day with those who happened to be there. A group of Epicurean and Stoic philosophers began to debate with him. Some of them asked, "What is this babbler trying to say?" Others remarked, "He seems to be advocating foreign gods." They said this because Paul was preaching the good news about Jesus and the resurrection. Then they took him and brought him to a meeting of the Areopagus, where they said to him, "May we know what this new teaching is that you are presenting? You are bringing some strange ideas to our ears, and we would like to know what they mean." (All the Athenians and the foreigners who lived there spent their time doing nothing but talking about and listening to the latest ideas.)

Paul then stood up in the meeting of the Areopagus and said: "People of Athens! I see that in every way you are very religious. For as I walked

around and looked carefully at your objects of worship, I even found an altar with this inscription: to an unknown god. So you are ignorant of the very thing you worship—and this is what I am going to proclaim to you" (Acts 17:16-23).

Paul was tactful, but he did not apologize for saying that the gods of the Greeks were no gods at all, or for proclaiming to them the true God and his plan.

Our mission is the same as Paul's. In looking at eastern mysticism, we hope to open the doors to the understanding of not only these other religions, but most importantly to better understanding of the true faith, by comparison.

A number of the mystical religions and cults in America are built on the foundations of Hinduism and Buddhism.

Hinduism

Hinduism is largely confined to India, where it is difficult to distinguish it from Indian culture itself. In fact, Sanskrit, the classical language of India and Hinduism, has no word for religion. To Hindus, religion is culture and vice versa.

It is even harder to get a grasp on Hinduism because it has no hierarchies, no rolls of membership, no congregations, sacraments, creeds, initiatory rites, or absolute practices. It is, as Alfred C. Lyall put it, "The absence of system...the wandering beliefs of an intensely superstitious people...a conglomerate of rude worship and high liturgies, of superstitions and philosophies belonging to very different phases of society and mental culture."[49]

Some distinctive elements of Hinduism can be pointed to, however, and among the main beliefs are:

---

[49] Alfred C. Lyall, *Natural Religion in India* (Cambridge, University Press, 1891) 13.

Karma

Karma is the order and interrelatedness of all things. Hindu thought is that this present world is here because of a sequence of causes and effects, and thus everything sprang into physical reality. To the individual, this means that you are here because certain forces did you the unwelcome favor of taking you out of your generalized unconsciousness and making you deal with time and space and empirical, tangible realities.

Reincarnation

Incarnation, to the Hindu, refers to one's coming to be in a physical form, whether that form is animal, vegetable or mineral, and if animal, whether fly, frog or person. After one's first incarnation, he goes through successive reincarnations until he manages to get back to the un-incarnate state, which we would call the spiritual realm.

Don't be confused by the term "spiritual" or "spiritual realm." For the Hindu, this unification with the spiritual realm is quite different than in Christian thought. God, or gods, also referred to as Brahman, the collective consciousness that brought things into being, is/are occasionally incarnated, resulting in great prophets.

Liberation

What would have to be called the Hindu concept of salvation is roughly the idea of liberation, which for the Hindu means escaping this present world by "eating up" his karma. This means to counteract the causes for his very *being* and thus reverse the process and enter the state of pure consciousness, which, it turns out, means more to be unconscious than to be conscious.

Troy Organ, in his book, *Hinduism,* says, "One of the aims of the Hindu is to exhaust his karma... each individual is accountable for his own life, and salvation from karmic causes of his embodiment is his own responsibility."[50]

It is clear from these few particulars that Hinduism is basically a negative religion or way of life. How much this sense of futility or pessimism is the result of the ancient, historic and typical poverty of India is debatable. But the obvious first cause is the rejection of the Biblical truth that life is good; that it is sin, not life itself, that is to be overcome; and that we live but once on this earth, and then comes the judgment (Heb. 9:27).

The sin of the pre-flood world was characterized by direct contradiction of revealed truth and by outright, declared rebellion against God's sovereignty. Hinduism is a culture/religion developed with this opposition principle central in its teaching. The result is a pessimism and a defeatism that is damaging not only to the individual, but to the ongoing culture in every way.

India is running over with well-fed cows, when controlling the population of cattle could relieve much starvation. Hinduism rejects the truth of God, which long ago gave us animals for food in the covenant with Noah.

India has many starving people. It has been popular to blame poor government policies or over-population. Those factors do contribute to the problem. But a major factor is Hinduism, which holds that all animals possess something of "the divine," and consequently most Hindus will not kill any animal for food.

Americans are most familiar with this concept from the Hindu's worshipful treatment of cows. Every twenty-four hours, one cow eats what would be for a human being several days worth of grain. India is running over with well-fed cows, when controlling the population of cattle could relieve much starvation. Hinduism rejects the truth of God, which long ago gave us animals

---

[50] Troy Wilson Organ, *Hinduism* (Woodbury, NY, Barrons Educational Series, 1974) 27.

for food in the covenant with Noah. While ultimately that will change, for the present it is part of God's plan for man's sustenance.

This is one of the most serious problems caused by pagan ideas. One Indian who has risen above his Hindu background says, "We are a thoroughly melancholic race—you may euphemistically call it mystic. Our sense of humor, if we have any, is very weak. Life is looked upon as an unwelcome burden, never as a privilege."[51] Another Indian comments, "A very large part of what is called Hindu thinking is wooly speculation or just mush."[52]

India is so closely aligned with Hinduism that the two are almost inseparable—in fact, the very names of the country and the religion come from the same root. Almost as closely united are the culture of China and the religion that is the heir to Hindu thought:

Buddhism

Buddhism has been described as relating to Hinduism in a similar manner as Christianity does to Judaism. The early cultures of India and China were compatible, and their religious ideas were shared. Buddhism has its origins in the time of Gautama the Buddha, who died in 545 B.C. Buddha means "the awakened one," and it was a title given to Gautama much in the same way that "Christ" is applied to Jesus. Gautama is called the Buddha because of his supposed experience of attaining what all Hindus and Taoists hope for: liberation from *maya*—the slavery to karma. Buddhists consider man to be enslaved to the forces that got him here to begin with, and thus they need liberation. According to Buddhist thought, there are Four Noble Principles to be accepted:

---

[51] Attributed to Madan Gopal, source unknown.

[52] Nirad Chaudhuri, an Indian writer, awarded an honorary Degree in Letters in 1990.

Duhkha

Duhkha means "suffering." To the Buddhist, the world is by nature a place of trouble. *Life* is trouble, a problem, a thing we must suffer through.

Trishna

Trishna means "grasping." Through trying to hold on to this world, we experience frustration. We are bound to karma, and doomed to repeat the cause of our existence, and so continue to exist here, until we have learned not to grasp.

Nirvana

Nirvana means "de-spiring." This basically means breathing out, not in; exhaling—not air from the lungs but thought from the mind, consciousness from the body. The aim of life is to achieve cessation of the turnings of the mind.

Nirvana may be pictured as the reverse of the process of condensation. Water vapor condenses and becomes tangible. If our lives were the droplets, Nirvana would mean we would aim to evaporate again, and join the vast vapors of water in the air.

God, to the Buddhist, is not an individual, not a person, not *personal* in fact, but a collective consciousness. He is not personally involved, but is rather like an automated industry, controlling himself and all processes.

Dharma

Dharma means "escape" We may achieve Nirvana by escaping karma. This involves a plan of meditation and disciplines which for the Buddhist include, formally, eight steps, including concentration on widening his view of the world, learning how to un-focus his mind, and training himself instead to focus on everything in general and nothing in particular.

Buddhist beliefs about the nature of God and the nature of man differ significantly from Christian concepts:

God. God, to the Buddhist, is not an individual, not a person, not *personal* in fact, but a collective consciousness. He is not personally involved, but is rather like an automated industry, controlling himself and all processes.

Man. Man, for the Buddhist, has no soul or spirit, since he is seen as a pinpoint extension of the cosmic consciousness. His goal, then, is not to make the most of individuality, but to lose it, to depersonalize and generalize, until he fades into virtual oblivion, oneness with the universal spirit which is Brahman, or god.

The themes of both Hindus and Buddhists run through the texts that are sacred to them, chiefly the Bhagavad Gita, the Vedas and the Upanishads, and the Buddhist "sutras." Most westerners are not inordinately attracted to Hinduism or Buddhism directly, the influence of Judaism and Christianity having been powerful in the development of western culture for the past 2,000 years.

However, various social movements of the 1960s and following years introduced eastern mysticism to new generations of westerners. As options for those who had become disillusioned with prevailing religious ideas, Hinduism and Buddhism gained some following in the United States, which continues into the 21st century.

Against the backdrop of these persistent, ancient religions, we now look at some of their modern variations.

Krishna Consciousness

Krishna Consciousness, what many people call Hare Krishna, is essentially an example of a Hindu missionary effort in the West.

There are a few accommodations to western thought, mostly in the designation of a personal side to the godhead. One spokesman for the Krisna movement says, "By chanting Hare Krishna, dancing in ecstasy, eating Krishna pasadam and reading books of transcendental knowledge such as Bhagavad Gita ("As It Is"), one can easily revive his dormant, loving relationship with Krishna, the Supreme Personality of Godhead, and thus attain the perfection of life in eternity, knowledge and bliss." If you have thought that it seems the main thing Krishna devotees are interested in doing is chanting and dancing, you were right; with the addition of rather involved dietary restrictions—vegetarian.

A work called the Hare Krishna Cookbook says, "Devotional service begins with the chanting of the Lord's holy names as in the maha mantra: (Hare Krishna, Hare Rama, etc.). That is the first great activity of *transcendental* service, and the next is to prepare and offer food to the Lord. The devotees of the Lord are released from all sins because they eat food that is offered first for sacrifice." This is pure Hinduism, transplanted into Western cultures. Very few Americans become members of the Hare Krishna sect. Studies of those who do often reveal that their reasons are rooted in psychological problems and/or spiritual struggles.

But for those looking for alternatives to Christianity and whose tastes run a bit more European, there is

Baha'ism

The Baha'i movement dates to 1844, when a Persian by the name of Mirza Hasayn Ali took the name Baha'u'llah, which means "the Glory of God," and announced he was the new incarnation of God, fulfilling Matthew 16:27 and other religion's expectations of a Messiah, Mahdi or other forthcoming Messiah. His Son Abdul-Baha and great grandson Shoghi Effendi carried on the movement, and Baha'i grew to be a worldwide reality. The International Baha'i Temple is in Haifa, Israel, and the United States location is in Wilmette, Illinois.

The doctrines of Baha'i include:

All religions are one
To the follower of Baha'i, followers of all religions worship the

same God, have the same roots (this is an interesting confession), and teach facets of the same ultimate truth.

Jesus has been replaced by Baha'u'llah

In fact, all predecessors of Baha'u'llah are replaced by him—none are negated, but all surpassed. (If it is interesting that Baha'i includes Jesus in the general superstructure of its tenets, it must be said that Pure Hinduism regards Jesus and other great men as incarnations of god or Brahman.)

Mankind is One

Baha'is stress the need to eliminate all forms of racism and discrimination.

The teaching of unity is largely responsible for the success of Baha'i in this divided and tired world. For instance, people find fault with Christianity for its many divisions and denominations, and for many of them that observation is the perfect excuse to refuse to listen to Christian witness. But most people's suggestions for unity under a single doctrine involve either compromise or replacement—in the case of Baha'i, mostly the latter.

Baha'is ignore the necessity of redemption through Christ, pass by sin as a real problem, do not believe in God as a loving Father, and do not accept the absolute Lordship of Jesus Christ. Strictly speaking, one cannot be a Baha'i and be a Christian—the faiths are mutually exclusive.

There is plainly implied pantheism in Baha'i doctrine (God is in everything), and what Abraham Kuyper calls "The irresistible tendency of our age to change along every line the God/man into the Man-god." Baha'i is clearly Hinduism, with mild accommodations to western ideas to soften the culture shock resulting from accepting Hinduism.

Still, many Americans are not only *not* interested in Oriental religions and their variants, but not interested in religion at all—so they say. For them, there is yet a variation on Hinduism which even some of the most scrupulously irreligious have taken up:

Transcendental Meditation

Teachers and students of Transcendental Mediation, often referred to simply as "TM," insist that it is not a religion, but simply a technique. But it must be remembered that to an Indian, Hindu is not a religion, but simply his way of life, his technique of life, if you please. TM is in the same class of activities—it suggests and leads to a way of life that can only be described as Hindu. After having discussed Hinduism, what does this definition of TM sound like?

According to Denise Denniston and Peter McWilliams, teachers of the TM method, "The Transcendental Meditation technique is a simple, natural process that allows the mind to experience subtler and subtler levels of the thinking process until *thinking is transcended* and the mind comes into direct contact with the *source of thought*" (emphases ours).[53] The key words and concepts of TM, to say nothing of the words, "transcendental meditation" themselves, give a positive identification: TM is Hinduism masquerading as a folk-technique for coping better with life.

There are doubtless other versions of Hinduism and Buddhism imbedded in our culture, or making their way into it. It is the concern of church leaders everywhere that Christians not be misled by eastern mysticism and not become even peripherally involved with groups or activities that instill Hindu ideas in their participants.

It also is the mandate of every true disciple of Jesus Christ to prepare to share the gospel of Christ with the Hindu, the Buddhist, the Baha'i, the Hare Krishna, on our shores and overseas. What does a Hindu or a follower of any of its variations need to hear?

---

[53] Denise Denniston and Peter McWilliams, *The TM Book* (Allenpark, MI, Versemonger Press, 1975) 36.

- *Scriptural authority.* First, he needs to face the question of the authority of revelation—the Bible. The beginnings of the revelation to the patriarchs and the Hebrew people predate any scriptures of other religions. *God was revealing himself* to the family of the first couple, and to their children, and guiding them into truth long before those wandering eastward fell into error.
- *The hard fact of sin.* Second, he needs to hear that it is the sin of man, and not man's existence, that needs to be overcome. *Man needs to repent* and needs a personal experience of regeneration, not reincarnation, by which he becomes a new person inside, and has hope of a very personal eternity with a very personal and loving God.
- *Christ the Savior.* Third, he needs to hear how God provided for that rebirth through the sending of his eternal Word Incarnate, whom we know as Jesus. *Jesus is The Christ, not A Christ,* and it was only by his substitutionary death that our sin was paid for, and only by his rising that eternal life was secured for each of us who will receive him as Lord into our lives.
- *Rely on the Holy Spirit.* Fourth, remember that even if discussions of the radical differences between mysticism and Christianity seem to go nowhere, the gospel *still* has the power to convict people of their sin and convince them of the truth, if God is working through his witnesses.

Summing up

One of the most important things of all is to present to the world an example of the victorious Christian, who enjoys life, who has not just serenity, but true peace—not just placidity, but full joy. In the scripture quoted at the top of this chapter, it is evident that Paul went joyfully and confidently and powerfully into Athens and dared to tell them of the God they had missed, the one they did not even know about. Because he went, there were some there that day who came to know the unknown God.

Perhaps, through you, someone in your life will also come to know the God who has revealed himself in history, in the Bible, and most of all in Jesus Christ.

Occultism
Detestable Practices
(Deuteronomy 18:9-13)

The Latin word *occultus* means "concealed, hidden or secret." The English word "occult" comes from this Latin root through the French "occulte." "The occult" refers to a quasi religious group of practices and beliefs, intended to "tap in," so to speak, to powers or forces that lie beyond everyday human life, in order to use those forces for purposes in this world.

Absolutely nothing positive can be said about occult practices. Nothing relating to truth or righteousness recommends them.

Things associated with the occult are not just "unwise" to be involved in, but manifestly sinful. At the outset, then, we need to be mindful of God's word on the subject. Of the many passages speaking of occult practices, perhaps the tersest, most final, and most compact is Deuteronomy:

When you enter the land the Lord your God is giving you, do not learn to imitate the detestable ways of the nations there. Let no one be found among you who sacrifices his son or daughter in the fire, who practices divination or sorcery, interprets omens, engages in witchcraft, or casts spells, or who is a medium or spiritist or who consults the dead. Anyone who does these things is detestable to the Lord, and because of these detestable practices the Lord your God will drive out those nations before you. You must be blameless before the Lord your God (Deuteronomy 18:9-13 NIV)

In 1852, Charles Mackay, author of "Popular Delusions and the Madness of Crowds," wrote concerning witchcraft as representative of occult practices, "It is consoling to think that the delirium has passed away; that the raging madness has given place to a milder folly; and that we may now count by units the votaries of a superstition which in former ages numbered its victims by tens of thousands, and its votaries by millions."[54] That was before the twentieth century revival of spiritism; and now, once again there are tens of thousands of victims, and millions of followers, engaged in all sorts of practices that fall under the general heading of the occult.

Moses listed the occult practices of his day, and he solemnly warned God's people against involvement in them. It is interesting to note that there is nothing basically new in the occult, despite the innovative twists that appear from time to time. So the ancient word of God is very much up to date, and plainly instructs us to avoid the occult entirely, and to warn others against it.

There is nothing basically new in the occult, despite the innovative twists that appear from time to time.

The occult is a broad field, and it is impossible to deal with all aspects of it completely in the space of one chapter; but looking at all the varieties at once will help us to understand what many of us miss: the occult is an interrelated field. Each type of occult practice relates to each of the others in a sinister way, by ties of principle, purpose, and source.

The Family of the Occult

The more you find out about the occult, the more you realize that the practices Moses listed for the Israelites, which are the same things going on today, are all a part of a big family. The principle behind this family of pursuits is the idea of the existence of spirit forces, either human or non-human. The purpose that binds the family together is to gain control over human affairs through the use of these forces.

---

[54] Charles Mackay, *Extraordinary Popular Delusions and the Madness of Crowds* (New York, Harmony Books, 1980) 564.

That would be the human statement of purpose. But the real purpose is to be understood from the perspective of the source of the occult, which is Satan. From his perspective, the purpose is not for people to get control over spirit forces, and thus their world, but for *him and the other evil spiritual beings* to get control over people. And the occult is very effective for Satan in this purpose.

The modern popularity of the occult in America is the result of a revival of spiritism, which can be dated to March 31, 1848, when two girls, Margaret and Kate Fox, began communicating with spirits in their farmhouse in Hydenville, N.Y., by means of mysterious clicks. The town, then the state, and then the country, were buzzing with curious excitement over this mysterious phenomenon, and similar mysteries began to spring up all over, in various forms.

The varieties of occultism today are almost too numerous to list, but their revival in our times springs from the explosion of spiritism in the last century.

Spiritism (or Spiritualism)

Spiritism is the belief that the spirits of the dead continue to exist all around us, that they can be communicated with, and that they can affect the lives of other persons. Spiritists believe that spirits have spiritual bodies and can occasionally materialize in this realm, especially through the aid of persons who have strong psychic power, called mediums.

Spiritists do not believe in heaven and hell as such, but they do believe that a person's life here affects his condition "on the other side," where all spirits strive to be elevated to higher levels of existence, which are considered to be at greater distances from the earth.

There is no belief in sin as the Bible teaches it; there is therefore no belief in the need of forgiveness, or a Savior.

Generally, spiritists claim that Abraham, Moses, Saul, Samuel, Isaiah, Daniel and Paul were psychics, and they say that Jesus was the greatest medium of all.

Spiritism involves seances (which may be called something else), in which people attempt to call up spirits of the dead, for various purposes.

During the revival of spiritism in the 1800s, the National Spiritualist Association of the USA was organized, and by 1923 it claimed 126,000 members, with 682 "churches" and 600 "ministers." By 1945 membership had grown to 228,000 members. Thousands of books on spiritism have been printed; two of the best known are *The Unobstructed Universe,* and *The Betty Book,* by Stewart White. In the latter, White records the supposed revelations of his dead wife, Betty, who says, "The only rock is recognition of the creator as greater than the thing created; acceptance of the oneness of consciousness as a whole." This is pantheism, and it is typical of the beliefs of spiritists.

Arthur Conan Doyle (author of Sherlock Holmes) was a spiritist. He bluntly stated that the ideas of the fall of man and the need of redemption are preposterous, and that there is no hell and no great gulf fixed between it and heaven.

Spiritists have no creed as such, but in general they are observed to believe:

1. That there is no personal God;
2. That there is no one Christ;
3. That spirits of the dead are purified through remorse for their evil deeds, and
4. Some spiritists have admitted believing that the Devil is the father of spirits with whom they seek to communicate.

The Bible clearly says, "Let no one be found among you...who is a medium or spiritist or who consults the dead."

The reason is easily discernable. Isaiah wrote, "When men tell you to consult mediums and spiritists, who whisper and mutter, should not a people inquire of their God?" (Isaiah 8:19 NIV). Spiritism is a radical diversion of a person from seeking God.

Even the slightest involvement compromises doctrine.

Theosophy

Theosophy is the broader philosophy behind spiritism and dozens of other occult practices. Essentially, theosophy is a marriage of spiritist practice with Buddhist theology. It is the belief that god is all and all is god.

Theosophists believe:

1. That modern history has been preceded by many other histories—i.e., before Adam—such as the Atlantean period (the belief in a continent called Atlantis);
2. In reincarnation;
3. That all men are brothers;
4. That one religion is as good as another; and
5. That the goal of life should be to gain knowledge of the spirit world and of the life beyond, and to escape this life eventually.

The problems with these beliefs are many.

Brotherhood. It may come as a surprise to people with only a modicum of Christian knowledge, but Jesus *did not* teach that all men are brothers; he taught that "My mother and brothers are those who hear God's word and put it into practice" (Luke 8:21), which means that only those who are united in him as doers of the will of the Father are brothers. The New Testament's word "brethren," or "brothers" (as in Acts 6:3, 2 Corinthians 1:8, 1 Thessalonians 5:1, 2 Thessalonians 1:3, etc.), refers to people united by faith in Christ.

Afterlife. The Bible teaches that there is one and only one way to God and his heaven: Jesus Christ.

Sin and salvation. Over and over the scriptures teach us that all have sinned, and all are dead in sin unless made alive in Christ through an experience of repentance and trust in him.

The Rosicrucians are theosophists. Their advertisements

appear in magazines and pulp newspapers, luring readers with the promise of learning the secrets of the universe and of mind power. There are many other organizations and fraternal orders throughout the world that go by innocuous names, but that espouse theosophistic beliefs.

Many fraternal orders shamelessly include the occult in their rituals and steps, placing power and significance in the ancient and superstitious symbols of Egyptian and Middle Eastern paganism, and bestowing honor upon the error of the past by perpetuating it. Many Christians have fallen for these things, believing them to be related somehow to true faith.

Many fraternal orders shamelessly include the occult in their rituals and steps, placing power and significance in the ancient and superstitious symbols of Egyptian and Middle Eastern paganism.

Divination

Divination is a class of arts or practices whose purpose is to find out the future, or discover secrets, by interpreting some material thing or things. Here is a list of the major types of divination:

Astrology. Astrology is the most popular and widespread divination practice. Today's astrology is the belief that the stars' and planets' position at the time of our births determined our personalities, and that their positions all through our lives affect events, both in a personal and a national-international way.

This belief has a long history. It began in ancient Chaldea, where primitive astronomers attempted to combine their observations of the movements of stars with their religious ideas. They constructed an imaginary belt in the heavens containing the stars and planets. They divided this belt into twelve sections, giving each a name by the principle constellation found in it. They called these the signs of the Zodiac.

Since it was believed that gods controlled the stars, it was concluded that they used them to control men's destinies. Thus, the sign you were "born under" was believed to have a lot to do with what kind of person you were and what would happen to you.

Modern astrology doesn't usually include a belief in the involvement of "gods." In a way, that omission makes it even less reasonable to think that stars have anything to do with human personalities. Yet just in America, at least five million persons plan their lives according to astrological predictions.

Mircea Eliade, in her book on occultism, gives us the figures: More than 1200 of the 1750 daily newspapers in the country publish horoscopes; an estimated forty million Americans participate in some way—more than 10,000 of them as full-time practitioners— in making astrology a 200 million dollar a year industry — just in this country![55]

Yet, it does not take much to discredit astrology—even without the commandments of God. To begin with, three planets have been discovered since the formation of the zodiac. And, due to the shift in the planets and stars in relation to earth (which is called precession) the signs of the zodiac are not even what they used to be: Virgo is now Libra, and so on down the list.

Astrology is based on the Ptolomaic conception of an earth centered universe. So much for that. Kenneth Boa, a Christian and an authority on cults and world religions, says, "Astrologers ignore most of the pertinent astronomical, biological and other scientific data now available. Astrology is a simplistic and stylized game far removed from the astronomical realities of the universe."[56]

Horoscopes often conflict with each other, and they typically offer advice that is so general in nature that it could apply to any

[55] Mircea Eliade, *Occultism, Witchcraft and Cultural Fashions* (Chicago, University of Chicago Press, 1978) 59.
[56] Kenneth Boa, *Cults, World Religions and You* (Wheaton, IL, Victor Books, 1979) 125)

sign, and be interpreted as meaning just about anything the reader wants. They have a character much like that of the so-called prophecies of Nostradamus, an astrologer, of whose predictions Charles Mackay has said, "A little ingenuity…might easily make events to fit some of them."[57]

But the most damning testimony against astrology comes from the word of God, which says in Isaiah 47 that its predictions have no meat or truth, and that all its counsel just "wears you out."

In spite of all this, many Christians have been duped into following horoscopes. Many believe them to be harmless. They read the predictions for their signs out of what they call curiosity. Those who visit astrologer-practitioners waste money on manipulative psychology from scam artists, reinforcing their gullibility.

In following such things a person opens a door in his life to the entrance of spiritual error, which is intimately tied to the worst of the occult. If the Bible means anything to the Christian's life and belief, he cannot escape the clear prohibition of the scriptures against astrology. It is divination, and God calls it "detestable."

Fortune Telling. The New Age Movement that began in the 1970s spawned a new generation of the familiar spiritism and theosophy of the previous century. This renovated occultism included a special place for angels and masters, beings believed to be able to communicate with human beings through meditation and ritual. The already established occult "readers" were augmented by practitioners claiming to be able to put people in touch with these spiritual beings for the purpose of guidance or healing.

Sister Fatima out on the highway with the sign that says, "Reader-Adviser" is no different from the ancient necromancers; modern fortune tellers use palms, tea leaves, crystals, or one of

---

[57] Mackay, 286.

hundreds of other methods, to predict the future or uncover secrets about the people who consult them.

There is very little that needs to be said about fortune tellers—the new age term is the more familiar, "counselors," —except that there is no authority behind their "wisdom." It is all an example of the gnostic idea that there is secret knowledge to be had in the magical arrangement of things or the channeling of spirit beings.

Many diviners attribute the forms of their tools of interpretation to the workings of spirits. The Bible calls these "familiar spirits," which means spiritual beings supposed to be at the beck and call of the medium. Fortune tellers are often mediums and hold seances—whether or not they call them by that name these days. Again, scripture specifically forbids us to "interpret omens."

Some people don't see the difference between fortune telling and what the Bible calls prophecy. The similarity owes to the fact that divination is a counterfeit of true prophecy.

- The prophet listens to the voice of God; the diviner to a familiar spirit, which is not God. The diviner will ultimately be surprised to learn this spirit was not a person who died but a demon, if anything more than his own imagination.
- The prophet forecasts events relating to God's work and kingdom; the diviner, of all sorts of miscellaneous events that people want to know in order to affect their personal prosperity.
- The true prophet has never been wrong, because it is God who speaks through him; the diviner is usually wrong, but it is his coincidental success that is advertised.
- The prophet worships God according to all scriptural revelation; the diviner rejects the truth of scripture and leads his customers down the same road.
- The prophet and the fortune teller are worlds—eternal worlds—apart.

Tarot. Tarot, or Tarot cards, go back centuries, and their readers are like fortune tellers in every respect, except that Tarot readers typically address questions to the pack before shuffling and reading. Who do you think answers?

While many people think this superstition is harmless, it is in fact quite dangerous. Many people do not think there are such things as demons, evil spirits, or even Satan. But there are, and it is just this disbelief that leaves people open to the work of these spirits when they dabble in superstitious things "just for fun."

Paul said, "Take your stand against the Devil's schemes. For our struggle is not against flesh and blood, but against the rulers, against the authorities, against the powers of this dark world and against the spiritual forces of evil in the heavenly realms" (Ephesians 6:11-12 NIV).

Over against diviners, there is another class of the occult, which raises more curiosity in the modern world than any other mystery:

Psychics

Psychic phenomena incorporate, again, a broad range of things, including several main categories, which we might call the three s's:

Sleuths. Some people claim to have extra sensory perception (ESP) by which they are able to read thoughts, solve mysteries, locate objects, etc. This is a shadowy area of investigation, and some scientists take it quite seriously. Many police departments have employed psychic sleuths in investigations, with a mixed bag of results. The CIA is currently spending money to look into using ESP, if possible, in covert operations. (Perhaps they'll call it ESPionage!)

Surgeons. Some persons claim to be able to perform psychic surgery without instruments and without leaving scars. Almost all such things have been proven to be slick and cruel trickery.

Spoon Benders. A whole class of psychics has arisen claiming to have enough mind power to affect inanimate objects. The "scientific" word for such practices is "psychokinesis." In a previous generation, Uri Geller made a hit bending spoons and moving clock hands. Yet Geller and others of his bent have been debunked by scientists, stage magicians and other investigators, who have discovered their tricks. Geller, by the way, claimed to have a power bestowed on him by a spaceship from the planet Hoova, which was hovering out in space somewhere near the earth.

The psychic's method involves the central idea of allowing the mind to be both concentrated and open. It is that openness that leaves the mind and spirit vulnerable to influences far deeper and more dangerous than the psychic imagines.

Most of these examples do not sound like the occult so much as they sound like a new twist on magic shows. But the character is still that of the occult. The psychic does not typically relate his performance to "spirits" or "gods," but there is a kinship of psychics with spiritist mediums, and the psychic's method involves the central idea of allowing the mind to be both concentrated and open. It is that openness that leaves the mind and spirit vulnerable to influences far deeper and more dangerous than the psychic imagines. Those influences are not mere energy fields; they are very personal forces. The Bible calls them demons; the chief of demons is Satan.

Two members of the occult family need to be considered:

Witchcraft
Witchcraft, or "wicca", often called "The Old Religion", is one of the most frightening forms of the occult. The word "witch"

means "one who knows", and refers to occult—hidden—knowledge (Gk. *gnosis)* that sets one apart.

In one form or another witchcraft has been around for quite a while; Moses specifically forbade it. Do not believe it if someone says, "There are no such things as witches." There may not be any wearing pointed hats and riding brooms as in fairy tales, but the number of real-life witches in the U.S. is reported by some news sources to be perhaps as high as 1.5 million. The reader might be startled to learn how many other things associated with witches in fantasy are actually a part of real witchcraft.

Witches are persons who call upon the elemental spiritual powers of the world to do things, and who make themselves available as hosts for these spiritual powers. Many witches claim they do only white magic (to benefit others) and not black magic (to hurt others.) But, as Kenneth Boa writes, "Witches desire to attain their own ends through the practice of their craft. They believe certain powers of evil affect the destinies of men and that the person who gets in contact with these powers can use them for his own purposes."[58]

Witches generally organize into covens, groups of a dozen or so, and meet for the observance of rituals and the casting of spells. This may sound fantastic and unbelievable to many of you, but it is all quite real. It has been going on for centuries. It's just that none of it is publicized or well known outside the covens themselves.

Because of the nature of the holiday, Halloween has become the high, holy day for witches around the world. What many parents think is just a time of fun for their children (and them) is actually a time rife with spells and incantations and the resulting demonic activity.

In the middle ages, the Templars were likely involved in witchcraft, as were a good number of priests in the Roman

---

[58] Boa, 112.

Catholic church. With the Inquisitions of the 16th and 17th centuries, witchcraft went underground, but it did not die. Drugs and nudity are a common part of typical, though not all, coven rituals, and the use of designs, incantations, and symbols that have traditional ties to demonic worship are standard. The witches code is "Do as thou wilt, an [if] ye harm no other. That is the whole of the *law.*"

USA Today recently interviewed J. Gordon Melton, a recognized expert in religions and the occult, and asked him to summarize the beliefs of witches. Here is what he said:

> "They worship a bisexual god. They see the deity as basically both male and female, with the female role predominant. They picture the female basically as the old Greek goddess, Diana, and her consort, Pan, the moon god. Sexuality has a very important role to play in witchcraft. They have picked up the reincarnation and karma from the East. They very much believe in cults and astrology. They worship out of the cycles of nature. They worship the earth mother, the sky god and focus on comings and goings of seasons. Their nature worship feasts are all based upon the agricultural season. Their regular worship is based upon the cycles of the moon. Their basic magical act is drawing down the moon—they gather in a circle, their sacred space, their temple, to 'raise the cone of power'—that is, they focus their emotional energy on something like a tornado cone; the magical act is to put that cone of power down into the group and then to use that power to work their magic."[59]

This desire to gain power over other people and material things, the appeal of mysterious adventure, or the attraction to

---

[59] J. Gordon Melton in *USA Today* (publication date not known)

sexual pleasure, have often led the witch to the final destination of all the occult:

Satan worship

If witchcraft is one of the more frightening aspects of the occult, Satanism is the *most* frightening. With their worship of the mother goddess and the horned god, their high rituals, forming the grand circle, raising the cone of power, brandishing knives and antique daggers, and often sacrificing animals in secret ceremonies, and calling directly upon the person of Satan, the Satanist and his cult can make you shudder to your bones. Boa says, "Satanism and witchcraft do not differ as much in kind as they do in degree. A witch may be uncertain about the source of power he or she is tapping but a Satanist freely acknowledges that the power comes from demons or from Satan himself."[60]

Satan worship is directed with full acknowledgment and full allegiance to Satan, whose devotees believe him to be willing to grant them power over people and things. There is some sort of contractual agreement undertaken, and those who call upon the power of Satan for their own ends understand implicitly that they are responsible to serve Satan in return.

Many people think the idea of signing away one's life to the Devil in blood was strictly fantasy out of the old tale of *The Devil and Daniel Webster,* but it really happens in Satan worship. Do not make the mistake of believing that those who do it are not *really* in league with the Devil. Persons who have been there and have, by the grace of God, been delivered and become Christians, tell us of the strange, horrifying things that go on in the Satanic covens, and of the genuinely demonic power that brings things to pass.

Satan worship is real. But thank God that it is not more powerful than what happens when a person yields his life to God! However terrifying Satan worship is, God is greater, stronger, and

---

[60] Boa, 13.

still in charge. That some who have actually worshiped Satan have since been converted is testimony to the power of God to turn a life around and make something holy out of something corrupt.

But the same attitude of disbelief that passes off Satan worship as so much myth, dismisses as innocent some of the direct reflections of Satan worship in our modern culture.

Such games as Dungeons and Dragons are *directly* tied to Satan and the occult. These role-playing games require openness to masters (called gods, deities, demons, etc.) and teach players how to serve them, and call upon them. Cartoons by the same name or variants on it—like Masters of the Universe, etc.—are milder versions of the same thing, which teach the same occult principles.

Ouija boards, which masquerade as games for both children and adults, are a common part of witchcraft and Satanist divination. They involve asking spirits to use the Ouija board to give an answer. Those "playing" the board are to allow unseen forces to move their hands. The boards can be, and are, used as a doorway to the occult.

All these objects and games open doorways to satanic influence at the very least.

Witnessing to someone involved in the occult?

- *Pray, pray, pray.* More than perhaps with any other witnessing encounter, you will be engaged in spiritual warfare when you try to talk about Jesus Christ with someone who dabbles in occult practices or actually worships Satan. Evaluate your own life; if you are relatively spiritually immature and you know it, seek help. Even if you are spiritually mature, do not assume that you will be successful. Submit your efforts to the Holy Spirit and count on him to work through his word.
- *Preparation.* If you have time in advance, do your homework about the specific form of the occult you are facing in your friend's life. If the opportunity comes but there's no time to prepare, stick to what you know and perhaps agree to talk

another time if the person is interested.

- *Scripture.* Remember that Jesus, when facing Satan in the wilderness, answered his temptations with scripture. The Christian's witness in similar confrontations needs to rely on the Bible for his answers, not just his own reasoning.
- *Holy Spirit.* Let God use his own word to bring conviction. It may happen for you, and it may not. Some sow seed, others cultivate it, and others may reap far down the way. Be content to do your part.

Summing up

From horoscopes to human sacrifice in the worship of Satan—it's all part of the family of the occult. Any and all of these things lead to one goal: the control of a person's life by the forces of evil. No matter how innocuous they may seem, this is their goal.

The writer of Proverbs, writing to those who did not see anything wrong with a little superstition here and there, said, "There is a way that appears to be right, but in the end it leads to death" (Proverbs 14:12 NIV). This is why God says, "You must be blameless before the Lord your God" (Deuteronomy 18:13 NIV). All these practices are "detestable" to him. All of them take a person *away* from God instead of leading them *to* him.

God wants people to fellowship with him, love him, and serve him. He knows that in the vain promises of necromancers, mediums, astrologers, or the unabashed invitations of Satan, there is only the promise of final destruction. God holds the key to a person's successful future; only he knows how to best solve their problems; only he can bring to their lives what will fulfil them; only he can make someone the kind of person he or she was made to be.

"When men tell you to consult mediums and spiritists, *should not a people inquire of their God?*" (Isaiah 8:19 NIV).

Unitarian Universalism
Vain Philosophy
(Colossians 2:8)

Two decades before the War Between the States, a fine preacher named Dr. Lyman Beecher dedicated himself to the preaching of the Bible in the region of Boston. It was an increasingly difficult field in which to serve, because of the influx of radical ideas. He therefore welcomed the coming of the famous evangelist from England, Charles G. Finney. But when Finney arrived, Beecher warned him that he would find his evangelistic work difficult, because, he said, "The Unitarians and Universalists have destroyed the foundation, and the people are all afloat."

Unitarianism continues today, and the beliefs espoused by Unitarians have had and do have an impact far beyond what they might on the surface appear to have had. In the study of other religions and cults in this country, we discover that Mary Baker Eddy, founder of Christian Science, was a Unitarian prior to her creation of her own religion. No less than five presidents of this country have been Unitarians. The Christian needs to know just what Unitarianism is.

Unitarianism was not around in Paul's day—not, at least, with a capital "U." But as the saying goes, the more things change, the more things remain the same. Paul covered a lot of bases in his teaching, and he covered what existed in his day as the roots of Unitarianism.

To the Church at Colossae Paul wrote:

See to it that no one takes you captive through hollow and deceptive philosophy, which depends on human tradition and the basic principles of the world rather than on Christ (Colossians 2:8 NIV).

Paul expounded and applied the teachings of the gospel as no other apostle of Jesus Christ. He was an educated man when he came to be a Christian, and he knew well what deceptions lie in the world of learning and culture. Here, as elsewhere, his warning to us is passionate: Don't be deceived!

Specifically, Paul explains the subtle dangers of a worldly, rationalistic approach to life and truth. Unitarian Universalism is a rationalistic philosophy that leaves out the perfect and exclusive revelation of God in the Bible and in Jesus Christ. It is precisely the kind of deception about which Paul warns all Christians.

After looking at Unitarianism in more detail, you will more firmly and knowledgeably believe the revelation of God in the Bible and in Christ Jesus.

Paul makes three main emphases in the verse above, which are precisely the focal points we want to notice in our inspection. The first of these is suggested by the phrase: "hollow and deceptive philosophy." Essentially, Paul's first condemnation of the religions or ideas to which he refers is that they make—

Reason the Rudder

The phrase as the apostle used it referred to the kind of rationalism promulgated in Greece by the philosophers who flourished there. Building on the approaches fostered by Plato and his kin, the Greeks constructed a system of life and thought in which everything was subjected to the dictates of "pure reason." However, Paul countered with two arguments: first, that it was arbitrary to discount revelation as a source of truth; and second, that the very reason exalted by philosophy is a sin-affected faculty of man, and performs faultily.

Philosophy or reason as the rudder of life is hollow because it leaves out the most important bulk of truth we have—that given by God through revelation. And philosophy is deceptive because with only partial knowledge—and that knowledge is flawed—we inevitably arrive at erroneous conclusions. This is the chief flaw of Unitarianism.

It isn't surprising that Unitarianism had its origins in the country that has now given us so-called higher Biblical criticism—

which is simply the subjection of the Bible to the rash dictates of over-bold reason. The Unitarian movement began as early as 1560, in Germanic Transylvania. Its basic ideas of the supremacy of reason as the guide of man found support in the spirit of the renaissance, and a growing movement in the reformation Church of England produced an actual secession of Unitarian groups.

At heart, the Unitarian movement was basically Arian — deriving from the theology of Arius, of the third and fourth centuries, who taught that Jesus was simply an exalted man—not one with God. This theology is arrived at by the application of the very kind of deceptive reasoning that Paul warned about.

The Unitarian movement gained momentum partly as the unfortunate result of a reaction to extreme Calvinism. The Unitarians, as others, found a wanted home in America, as their first church was established in Boston in 1785. An Episcopal congregation, sorely infected with the disease of rationalism, was wrenched from the fellowship of mainstream Christians when the congregation voted that year to become Unitarian. That same theme—the alteration of genuinely Christian institutions, is repeated time after time throughout Unitarian history since. In 1805, a Unitarian professor was appointed at Harvard, a school that had been founded more than a century before to train orthodox Christian ministers. Harvard's history since demonstrates the fruit of rationalism planted within evangelical Christianity.

Reason is the rudder to the Unitarians; but what an ineffective rudder it has been. Charles Finney found Dr. Beecher's words profoundly accurate, as he wrote in 1875:

> The mass of people in Boston are more unsettled in their religious conviction than in any other place that I have ever labored in, notwithstanding their intelligence: for they are surely a very intelligent people, on all questions but that of religion. It is extremely difficult to make religious truths lodge in their minds, because the influence of Unitarian teaching has been to lead them to call into question all the

principle doctrines of the Bible. Their system is one of denials. Their theology is negative. They deny almost everything, and affirm almost nothing. In such a field error finds the ears of the people open; and the most irrational views on religious subjects come to be held by a great many people.[61]

Finney hit at the very heart of the error of rationalists: the assumption that reason must exclude revelation. It does not make sense to think that the puny mind of man can arrive at all truth on its own. To define reason in such a way is *unreasonable*. God says that his ways and his truth are imminently reasonable.

In his introduction to the Old Testament "good news" about God's offer of forgiveness and cleansing from sin, Isaiah 1:18 the prophet wrote, "Come now, let us *reason* together, says the Lord." The gospel makes sense, in the most profound way.

It does not make sense to think that the puny mind of man can arrive at all truth on its own. To define reason in such a way is *unreasonable.*

The New Testament records in Acts 17:2, 17:17, 18:4, and 18:19 that Paul "reasoned" (18:19) with hearers concerning the deity and Messiahship of Christ and the truth of the resurrection.

And Hebrews 11:19 says, "Abraham reasoned that God could raise the dead." Reason must include God as a factor, or it becomes grossly incomplete.

Trying to live by reason, or construct theology by reason, without including the self-evident input of God himself, is like trying to ride a tricycle without the front wheel, or sail a ship

---

[61] Charles Finney, *The Autobiography of Charles Finney* (Minneapolis, Bethany Fellowship, 1977) 192.

without a steering mechanism. For the Unitarians, reason is the rudder, but their rudder is not connected to the pilot house.

How people could arrive at such a philosophy can only be explained by recognizing a second thing that Paul pointed out. God and his truth should be the apex of all our desire and the highest point of our aspiration—the standard by which all is judged. However, such vain philosophies as Unitarianism have made—

Humanity the High Point

We hear a lot in these times about humanism, sometimes called godless humanism, atheistic humanism, or secular humanism. Humanism simply means a focus on humanity, the primacy of man in human activities. The Unitarian stress on the supremacy of reason derives from the basic, proud attitude of humanism: putting man first in a world where God is to be acknowledged as supreme. The rudder of reason, and all successive doctrines of the Unitarians, proceed from this exaltation of humanity beyond its place. It places man in judgment of God's truth—and that puts man over God.

This relationship of Unitarians to humanism is well established in history. In May of 1961, the Unitarians and Universalists united by official vote to become the Unitarian Universalist Association. Three major faces to the rationalist movement in the world can be identified: Humanism, Modernism, and Unitarian-Universalism. They constitute a sort of unholy trinity in which Humanism is the omnipresent principle, Modernism is the widespread, ecumenical trend, and Unitarianism is an actual organization crystalizing the beliefs.

A short run-down of those beliefs will help to identify just what kind of modernism Unitarianism is:

Bible

The Unitarian's source of authority is not the Bible, but

reason—the mind of man. Therefore, the Bible is regarded not as *the* word of God, but as much an inspired book as are all the other so-called holy writings of all religions. Charles Elliot, a late president of Harvard, stated it this way: "We no longer depend for salvation upon either a man or a book. Men help us; books help us; but back of all stands our divine reason."

God

The derivation of the title "Unitarian" is the teaching that God is not trinity but unity. Unitarians deny that Christ is one with God. When it comes right down to it, however, their idea of God is basically pantheistic, making God personally present in all creation, and suspiciously united with the essence of man. This sort of God is not open to petition in the usual sense, and thus prayer is virtually a non-possibility. One Universalist minister writes, "Why pray? We ourselves must answer."

Christ

Jesus, though not God in the flesh, was, according to Unitarianism, a highly developed man, perhaps the greatest of teachers. But the idea of incarnation is scorned. Modernist theologian Reinhold Neibuhr sounds very Unitarian when he calls the incarnation "an offense to reason."

Resurrection

Naturally, if Unitarians do not believe Christ was the God-man, they deny the resurrection as well. Unitarianism asserts that the idea of bodily resurrection is a myth.

One Unitarian writer explains that the resurrection was the sudden perception of the disciples that life continues somehow beyond the grave. Just that, but no more. The logical result of their denying Christ's resurrection is that they also deny the resurrection of the saved at some future date. (For the Apostle Paul's argument on this matter, read 1 Corinthians 15:12-21.)

Harry Emerson Fosdick, admittedly a gifted speaker, and

admired by a frightening number of otherwise mainstream Christians, was a modernist and a virtual Unitarian, and said, "I believe in the persistence of personality through death but I do not believe in the resurrection of the flesh." Fosdick also stated, "I do not believe in the physical return of Jesus." This is a fair representation of the views of Unitarians on the second-coming.

Man

The Unitarian view of man is thoroughly humanistic. As a class, Unitarians and Modernists believe in evolution and firmly deny creation as it is presented in Genesis. Man is not fallen, they say, but only struggling to become, out of the incompleteness of his evolutionary origins.

Salvation

Salvation, then, is not something God does for man by a redemptive act, but something man does for himself through good works and the development of society and culture. Salvation is not viewed as being a matter of eternal consequence, but of temporal quality of life only. Because for the Unitarian-Universalist, everybody will be, or is, saved.

Originally, Universalists believed that in the end all would be saved by some act of universal inclusion. Now, they embrace the more the general idea that there is no need for salvation in the first place, thus, universal safety is a given. In fact, Unitarianism broadly disbelieves in hell, and mostly disbelieves in heaven.

If it seems that such beliefs lead downward in a sort of spiral to a point at which not much is believed in at all, that is precisely the point. Since the beginning of Unitarian Universalism, this has been their direction. It is not difficult to conclude that it was their unconscious intention.

People can easily be caught up in a movement whose direction they are essentially unaware of. For Unitarians, the spirit of their error makes—

Godlessness the Goal

Really, nothing in Unitarianism demands retaining a concept of God, except that including him incidentally makes Unitarianism a bit more palatable to the average, uninformed man who likes to think he still believes in God. But the doctrine of Unitarianism is otherwise so unbiblical and devoid of true spiritual content that it does not need God to continue.

If it seems that such beliefs lead downward in a sort of spiral to a point at which not much is believed in at all, that is precisely the point.

Satan inspires such non-religion as this, and he is willing to have God around for prestige, as long as that is of value; but when it is no longer necessary for the sake of the religion's survival—the popularity of Humanism suggests such in the present day—God can be dropped.

Paul says such error as Unitarianism depends "on the principles of the world rather than on Christ." Here is the real condemnation of Unitarian Universalism: God is ignored, and man is enthroned. God is bypassed, and man is exalted.

Unitarians' rejection of God as the Bible reveals him is based on their exaltation of *reason over faith*. Where faith is taken to mean *blind* acceptance, dependence on reason might be called for, but biblical faith is not blind acceptance. It is *reasonable* dependence on the self-evident revelation of God in the course of biblical history. The great 11th chapter of Hebrews in the New Testament illustrates repeatedly from the Old Testament how faith was the response of people to the revelation of God, often in words delivered by the Angel of the Lord or in divinely given dreams or from the mouths of powerful prophets. The Unitarian's rejection of the way of faith is a rejection of the revelation of God in the scriptures.

The Christian's "dictionary" says this is what "faith" means:

- It means more than some sort of mental cognizance of a deity: it means the total occupation of a human being with his creator, placing him on the throne as Lord God Almighty.
- It means acceptance of what God reveals as truth, including belief in Jesus Christ as God-incarnate.
- It means trust in what God has revealed as the one and only way of entering into eternal life, which is personal acceptance of the life-payment of Christ Jesus for our sin, and a turning of our lives away from that sin and unto him.
- It means, in short, that Christ, the Son of God, is all in all to us, and that we consider ourselves eternally as well as temporally dependent upon him, or lost without him.

If witnessing to a Unitarian Universalist

- *On the offensive.* Remember that the Unitarian's religious milieu is reason and rationalism. Avoid resorting to merely reasonable argument: use the scriptures. Stay on the offensive.
- *Probe eternal realities.* The Unitarian may not have any real expectation of eternal life, or may assume that some sort of heaven is the destination of everyone. Repeat Jesus' teachings about heaven and hell and find out if your Unitarian friend would really like to have assurance about his future.
- *Personal testimony.* Intersperse your discussion with personal experience of Jesus Christ. The Unitarian's experience of his or her own "faith" will be lacking in any deeply fulfilling encounter with God. Let them see yours and sense that it is real.
- *Spiritual reliance on God.* As with all witnessing encounters with people of any faith, your power must come from God. The Holy Spirit uses his own word to bring conviction and faith. Pray before, during and after witness. And don't be discouraged if your witness doesn't win someone on the spot. Many people, buried deeply in their own belief or unbelief and their own traditions, take much time and perhaps unexpected

encounters with God to bring them to the acceptance of Christ.

Summing up

The foundational truths of the Bible are simple, and acceptance of them by faith is not unreasonable, but instead is a demonstration of the most profound kind of reason—the willingness to believe a reliable source: God.

The Bible says God created us for fellowship with him, but that sin in each of us has marred that fellowship and cut us off from him.

Since we cannot possibly save ourselves, the only remedy is redemption, through the incarnation, substitutional death, and actual resurrection of the God-man: Jesus Christ.

We are forgiven of sin, born anew to eternal life, and guaranteed bodily resurrection like Christ when we turn from self and sin and name Christ as Lord of all, in an act of faith in him.

This the word of God affirms; and *this* true Christians believe.

Bibliography

Baker, Robert. *A Summary of Christian History*. Nashville: Broadman Press, 1959.

Barnes, Fred. "Can We Trust the News?" In *Reader's Digest*. Jan. 1988, 37-38.

Boa, Kenneth. *Cults, World Religions and You*. Wheaton, IL: Victor Books, 1979.

Brantley, George. *Catholicism*. New York: G. Braziller, 1961.

Cox, Harvey. *The Secular City*. New York: Macmillan Publishing, 1990.

Crowther, Duane S. *The Godhead*. Springfield, UT: Horizon Publishers, 2008.

Denniston, Denise and McWilliams, Peter. *The TM Book*. Allenpark, MI: Versemonger Press, 1975.

Eliade, Mircea. *Occultism, Witchcraft and Cultural Fashions*. Chicago: University of Chicago Press, 1978.

En.Wikipedia.org. "The Matrix," Accessed January 1, 2023.

Finney, Charles. *The Autobiography of Charles Finney*. Minneapolis: Bethany Fellowship, 1977.

Gerstner, John H. *The Teachings of Christian Science*. Grand Rapids: Baker Book House, 1975.

Lippman, Thomas W. *Understanding Islam*. New York: Penguin Publishing Group, 1982.

Lyall, Alfred C. *Natural Religion in India.* Cambridge: University Press, 1891.

Mackay, Charles. *Extraordinary Popular Delusions and the Madness of Crowds.* New York: Harmony Books, 1980.

Mary Baker Eddy. *Science and Health with Key to the Scriptures.* Boston: W. F. Brown & Co. Printers, 1875.

Organ, Troy Wilson. *Hinduism.* Woodbury, NY: Barrons Educational Series, 1974.

Potter, Charles. *The Faiths Men Live By.* New York: Prentice Hall, 1954.

Robertson, A. T., *Word Pictures in the New Testament, Vol. 1.* Nashville: Broadman Press, 1930.

Rosten, Leo. *What is a Christian Scientist.* New York: Simon and Schuster, 1975.

Rosten, Leo. *Religions in America.* New York: Simon and Schuster, 1963.

Saints and the Baptist Witness. Nashville: Home Mission Board, SBC, 1975.

Schaeffer, Frances. *How Then Shall We Live.* Grand Rapids: Fleming H. Revell Co, 1976.

Smith, Huston. *The World's Religions.* San Francisco: Harper, 1991.

Tanquerey, Adolph. *The Spiritual Life.* Westminster, MD: The Newman Press, 1930.

The Christian Science Journal. New York: Christian Science Publishing Society, 1906.

Wikipedia.org. "Scientology." Accessed October 18, 2023.

Williams, John Alden. *Islam.* New York: George Braziller, Inc., 1961.

Zaimov, Stoyan. "Jews Are Saved Even Without Believing in Christ, Vatican Claims." In *The Christian Post,* October 18, 2023.

www.ingramcontent.com/pod-product-compliance
Lightning Source LLC
Chambersburg PA
CBHW030936090426
42737CB00007B/450